CHICAGO
IN YOUR POCKET

A handy directory of restaurants, hotels, museums, theaters, stores, nightlife, famous landmarks—the best of the city's sights, services, and pleasures!

Second Edition

BARRON'S

Woodbury, New York • London • Toronto
Sydney

Credits

Chicago subway map reprinted courtesy of the Chicago Transit Authority. Additional maps of Chicago reprinted courtesy of Chicago *Sun-Times*.

Book design by Milton Glaser, Inc.
Illustrations by Juan Suarez

All inquiries should be addressed to:
Barron's Educational Series, Inc.
113 Crossways Park Drive
Woodbury, New York 11797

International Standard Book No. 0-8120-2974-7

PRINTED IN THE UNITED STATES OF AMERICA

567   880   987654321

CONTENTS

Preface and Acknowledgments   7
Finding Your Way Around Town   9

Annual Events   9
Antiques   12
Art Events   13
Art Galleries   13
Art Supplies   16
Auctions and Flea Markets   16

Bakeries and Pastry Shops   17
Bargain and Discount Stores   17
Bars and Pubs   18
Beauty Shops and Barbers   19
Bed and Breakfast   20
Books About Chicago   20
Bookstores   21
Boutiques   24

Ceramics, China, Glass, and Pottery   26
Cheese Shops   27
Children and Children's Things   27
Chocolate and Candy   29
Coffee and Tea   30
Cosmetics   31

Dance   31
Department Stores   32
Drugstores   34

Ethnic Neighborhoods and Shops   34
Excursions Out of the City   36

Fabric Shops   37
Furs   38

Gay Scene   38
Gourmet Foods   42
Gyms and Indoor Sports Facilities   42

Haberdasheries   43
Hospitals and Health Emergencies   44
Hotels   45
Housewares and Cooking Utensils   49

Information   50

Jewelry Shops   51

Leather Goods and Luggage   52
Linens   52
Lingerie   53

Magic and Metaphysical   53
Movies   53
Museums   54
Music   60

Newspapers and Magazines   63
Nightlife   64

Contents

Parks and Nature Preserves 66
Perfume and Other Toiletries 66

Photography 67
Police and Emergencies 67
Prints and Posters 68

Racetracks 68
Records and Tapes 69
Religious Services 69
Rentals 69
Restaurants 71

Second-Hand Clothing/Thrift-Vintage 82
Shoes 83
Shopping Malls and Centers 83
Sights Worth Seeing 84
Specialty Shops 91
Sporting Goods 93
Sports 93
Stationery 95

Theaters 95
Things to Do 98
Tobacco 99
Tours and Sightseeing 100
Toys 101
Transportation 102

Universities 105

Weather 106
Wines and Liquors 106
Women's Interests 107

Zoos 107

Maps 109

    Downtown Chicago 109
    Metro Chicago 110
    Chicago—North/Northwest 112
    Downtown Chicago Subway—South inside back cover
    Downtown Chicago Subway—North inside front cover

PREFACE

You can't see the garage where the St. Valentine's Day massacre took place; it's been torn down. (You can, however, check out the alley where Dillinger was shot as he left the Biograph Theater.) The stockyards are gone, too, but the world's biggest commodities exchange lives noisily, thrivingly on.

And so does the rest of the city. Today Chicago is the home of skyscrapers, the blues, and deep-dish pizza. Nelson Algren, who lived and worked here most of his life, called it "a city on the make." That may still be true, but there is some sophistication now along with the hustle. The world's most acclaimed symphony orchestra and the nation's most outstanding collection of French impressionist paintings can be found here. Also, there's the world's tallest building, the busiest airport in the United States, and the famous eclectic mix of architecture: Louis H. Sullivan, Mies van der Rohe, Daniel Burnham, and Frank Lloyd Wright.

This book concentrates on the core areas of the city: the Loop, the Near North, and Lincoln Park. Other neighborhoods of interest and suburbs are included as well. Although every effort is made to keep information up to date, things do change. It's often wise to call first.

Acknowledgments

We gratefully acknowledge the help of Marcia Froelke Coburn and Susan Figliulo in researching and preparing the material for this book.

SEARS TOWER

FINDING YOUR WAY AROUND TOWN

Chicago streets are laid out in a grid pattern, which makes finding addresses fairly easy. The central point, or zero, is the intersection of Madison and State Streets in the Loop. All north-south street addresses grow larger as they move away from Madison; all east-west addresses grow larger as they move away from State Street.

A complete street guide is printed inside the *Chicago Yellow Pages Buying Guide*, the "B" phone book.

Chicago has a North Side, South Side, and West Side; the "East Side" is Lake Michigan. The downtown Loop area (its name comes from the loop the el train makes through it) is defined as south of Wacker Drive and the Chicago River to the Eisenhower Expressway. The Near North, which includes Michigan Avenue, runs north of the Chicago River to Division Street.

Other neighborhoods mentioned often in this book—Old Town, Lincoln Park, Lakeview—are farther north. Hyde Park is south of the Loop.

AIRPORTS

See TRANSPORTATION.

ANNUAL EVENTS

For the most up-to-date information, check the Special Events listing in *Chicago* magazine. Or call the Mayor's Office of Special Events, 744-3315.

January

Sometime between the last 10 days of this month and the first week of February, Chinatown celebrates its New Year. Chinatown is located at 22nd and Wentworth; call the Chinese Civic Council, 225-0234, for details.

February

Go to Lincoln Park Zoo on February 2 to see if the groundhog will spot his shadow. Presidents' Day Parade, a big political affair, takes place on or near February 12.

March

Early this month, the Annual Clarence Darrow Memorial Day is celebrated in Hyde Park by throwing a wreath into the river. Then on March 17, everyone's Irish. The river is dyed green; Chicago's biggest parade marches down Dearborn Street.

April

Check out the Easter Flowers Shows at the Garfield Park Conservatory, 300 N. Central, and the Lincoln Park Conservatory, Fullerton and Lincoln Park. Call 294-4770 for details.

May

Free noontime concerts start inside the Cultural Center, 78 E. Washington, and outside in the First National Bank Plaza, 38 S. Dearborn. Another springtime event that has become well established is the Art Expo, which attracts dealers and aficionados from all over the world.

June

The city's Neighborhood Festivals begin; they are often, but not always, ethnically oriented. Call 744-3315. Evening concerts can be heard around the band shell in Grant Park, Jackson and Columbus Drive.

Gay and Lesbian Pride Week, including a parade down Broadway, takes place the third week. For details, call Gay & Lesbian Switchboard, 929-4357. And Ravinia Park, the Highland Park outdoor concert park, opens its season. Concerts by the Chicago Symphony Orchestra—plus some pop attractions—are the summer bill. Transportation by the Chicago and Northwestern trains, 454-6677.

July

Tradition has it that almost everyone comes to Grant Park on July 3 for the annual concert and fireworks display. If you miss it, catch the fireworks in Soldiers Field on the 4th. The Taste of Chicago, over the 4th weekend, allows one to sample all the finest foods from Chicago's best restaurants, plus many ethnic goodies.

August

The lakefront is alive: the Lakefront Festival begins in the middle of the month; and then it's Venetian Night, one of Chicago's loveliest events. Venetian Night is delicately lighted yachts, water floats, and fireworks. Not to be missed, it's usually scheduled for the last Friday in August. Also, the Jazz Festival starts in Grant Park.

September

The Jazz Festival, with some of the biggest names, continues in Grant Park.

October

Everybody loves the Italian-American parade, on either October 12 or the second Saturday of the month.

November

Chicago's International Film Festival runs for 2 weeks at a variety of theaters; call 644-3400 for details. The International Folk Fair is also this month. And Santa's Fantasy Parade takes place the Sunday after Thanksgiving.

December

A beautiful display, called "Christmas Around the World," can be seen at the Museum of Science and Industry. And stroll down the State Street Mall to view the department stores' display windows.

ANTIQUES

Antique shopping or browsing is a well-established weekend pastime. Prime neighborhoods include: the 700 block of N. Wells; Belmont from 800 to 2500 west; and the shops around Halsted and Armitage. Most stores are closed on Mondays.

Antiquery Warehouse 2050 N. Halsted; 528-3121.
Brown Beaver Antiques 2600 W. Devon; 338-7372. Brass beds.
Donrose Galleries 751 N. Wells; 337-4052. Chicago's largest dealer. Specializes in furniture and Oriental art.
Elf Shoppe Antiques 846 W. Armitage; 935-4110. Victorian oak and walnut furniture.
Harvey Antiques 1231 Chicago, Evanston; 866-6766. Quality Early American and folk art.
Jay Roberts Antique Warehouse 149–55 W. Kinzie; 222-0167.
Mark & Lois Jacobs Americana Collectibles 2465 N. Lincoln; 935-4204. Political antiques and memorabilia; pop culture items.
O'Hara's Gallery 707 N. Wells; 751-1286.
Quercus Antiques 2148 N. Halsted; 281-2616.
Turtle Creek 850 W. Armitage; 327-2630. American primitive, wicker, and quilts.
Victorian House 806 W. Belmont; 348-8561.

ARCHITECTURE, ARCHITECTURAL SIGHTS

See SIGHTS WORTH SEEING.

ART EVENTS

Chicago holds 2 well-known art fairs every year: the Gold Coast Art Fair and the Old Town Art Festival. Check *Chicago* magazine or the Mayor's Office of Special Events, 744-3315, for scheduling.

ART GALLERIES

Galleries in Chicago are concentrated on N. Michigan Avenue and the surrounding side streets, with a large majority clustered in "Suhu," the up-and-coming Superior-Huron neighborhood. Most are open Tuesday–Saturday, 10 A.M.–5 P.M. During August, however, many galleries are closed.

ARC Gallery 6 W. Hubbard; 266-7607. Cooperative gallery founded by women offers the newest by the freshest.
Arts Club of Chicago 109 E. Ontario; 787–3997. Various exhibitions; a Mies van der Rohe interior.
B. C. Holland 224 E. Ontario; 664-5000. Specializes in sculpture.
DART 212 W. Superior; 787-6366. Contemporary art.
Dobrick Gallery 216 E. Ontario; 337-2002. Kinetic sculpture.
Douglas Kenyon Gallery 155 E. Ohio; 642-5300. Mainly photography.
Fairweather-Hardin Gallery 101 E. Ontario; 642-0007. Prints.

GROUNDS OF THE ART INSTITUTE

Frumkin & Struve 309 W. Superior; 787-0563. Contemporary art.

Gilman Galleries 277 E. Ontario; 337-6262. Paintings and sculpture.

Hokin-Kaufman Gallery 210 W. Superior; 266-1211. African primitives; contemporary art.

Jacques Baruch Gallery 900 N. Michigan; 944-3377. Eastern European art.

Joseph Faulkner Main Street Gallery 620 N. Michigan; 787-3301. Nineteenth- and 20th-century drawings and sculpture.

Landfall Press, Inc. 215 W. Superior; 787-6836. Lithographs.

Marianne Deson Gallery 340 W. Huron; 787-0005. Conceptual art.

Merrill Chase Galleries Water Tower Place, 835 N. Michigan; 337-6600. Posters, sculpture, expensive lithos.

Michael Wyman Gallery 233 E. Ontario; 787-3961. African art.

Mongerson Gallery 620 N. Michigan Avenue; 943-2354. Nineteenth- and 20th-century American-Western.

N.A.M.E. Gallery 9 W. Hubbard; 467-6550. Avant-garde.

Phyllis Kind Gallery 313 W. Superior; 642-6302. Lots of Chicago Imagists.

Printworks, Ltd. 311 W. Superior; 664-9407. Posters and prints.

Randolph Street Gallery 756 N. Milwaukee; 243-7717. Avant-garde; its holiday sale offers bargains on great gifts.

Renaissance Society 5811 S. Ellis; 962-8670. On the University of Chicago campus, this gallery shows fine modern art; watch for its Art for Young Collectors sale in November.

Richard Gray Gallery 620 N. Michigan; 642-8877. Contemporary.

R. S. Johnson, International 645 N. Michigan Avenue (entrance on Erie); 943-1661. Famous, well-respected gallery.

Samuel Stein 620 N. Michigan; 337-1782. Well-known artists represented with paintings, sculpture, graphics.

Van Straaten Gallery 361 W. Superior; 642-2900. Prints and paintings.

Wally Findlay Gallery 814 N. Michigan; 649-1500. Paintings by Chagall, Simbari, others.

ZAKS Gallery 620 N. Michigan; 943-8440. Large selection of Chicago artists.

Zolla/Lieberman Gallery 356 W. Huron; 944-1990. Mixed media.

ART MUSEUMS

See MUSEUMS—ART.

ART SUPPLIES

Aiko's Art Materials Import 714 N. Wabash; 943-0745. Specializes in Japanese art supplies.

Favor Ruhl 14 S. Wabash; 782-5737.

Flax Co. 176 N. Wabash; 346-5100.

Sheldon's 200 E. Ohio; 822-0900.

AUCTIONS AND FLEA MARKETS

Chicago Art Galleries 1633 Chicago, Evanston; 475-6960. Fine arts.

Flea Market at Belmont Hall 1635 W. Belmont; 549-9693. Indoor market open Saturday and Sunday, 9 A.M.–5 P.M.

Great American Flea Market 1333 S. Cicero, Cicero; 242-2045. Largest indoor flea market with over 250 booths.

Maxwell Street Halsted Street and 1320 South. A Chicago Institution of buying, trading, and haggling in the open street. It's seen finer days, but go on a Sunday morning and be prepared to be accosted by zealous merchants. Prices are to be dickered over, of course.

Auctions

Sotheby Parke Bernet 700 N. Michigan; 280-0185. Leading art auctioneers.

BAKERIES AND PASTRY SHOPS

See also ETHNIC SPECIALTY SHOPS.

Bon Ton Pastry Shop & Restaurant 1153 N. State Street; 943-0538. Small Hungarian restaurant renowned for its pastries.
Bread Shop 3400 N. Halsted; 528-8108. Suspiciously delicious whole-grain breads, other healthy treats.
French Baker 26 W. Madison; 346-3532.
Let Them Eat Cake 948 N. Rush; 951-7383. Closed Sunday and Monday.
Roberto Albini Bottega del Pane 121 E. Oak; 664-0963. Chic nuovo-Italiano specialties in the One Magnificent Mile building.
Vie de France Water Tower Place, 835 N. Michigan; 266-7633. Café and take-out. Croissants and French breads.

BARGAIN AND DISCOUNT STORES

Apparel Center 350 N. Orleans. This is the center for manufacturers' wholesale showrooms. A good place to pick up current fashions in sample sizes and display accessories on sale. Days and hours for the public are changeable.
Crate & Barrel Warehouse 1510 N. Wells; 787-4775. This store is devoted to cookware, housewares, modern crystal, and pottery—all at low prices. Everything is a second, odd lot, or closeout, in good condition.

Factory Handbag Store 1036 W. Van Buren; 421-4589. Factory overruns of leather purses, wallets, and belts; all prices at wholesale or lower.

Handmoor's 300 N. Michigan Ave.; 726-5600. Designer clothes and accessories at 20 percent or more off; lots of Calvin Klein sportswear, Gucci watches, and a huge coat department. Free limo service to and from Water Tower area.

Kroch's & Brentano's Bargain Book Center 62 E. Randolph; 263-2681. Closeouts on hardcovers and paperbacks.

Loehmann's Randolph and Wells; 346-7150. A smaller, but not necessarily less hectic, branch of the New York discount store. Women's apparel only.

Off-Center 300 W. Grand (at Franklin); 321-9500. This is an entire—all 6 floors—shopping center devoted to bargains. The stores here—and they tend to come and go—offer discounts of 25 percent and more. Merchandise was often seen in Michigan Avenue boutiques a few months earlier.

Outlet 2241 N. Elston; 382-4174. This is Land's End warehouse store. Bargains in sportswear, rugged outdoor wear, and accessories. Open only Friday, Saturday, and Sunday, 9 A.M.–5 P.M.

Regency Book Shop 200 S. State, 7th Floor; 786-9786. Usually 25 percent off best sellers; art books. Deliveries to Loop addresses.

BARS AND PUBS

Arnie's Bar 1030 N. State; 266-4800. Popular piano bar section of a restaurant. Decorated with an overdose of art deco.

Beaumont 2020 N. Halsted; 281-0177. Elegant neighborhood bar. Packed on Friday and Saturday nights.

Bentley's 801 W. Willow; 280-9126. Wine bar and gourmet snacks.

Billy Goat Tavern 430 N. Michigan Avenue, lower level; 222-1525. Popular with newspaper reporters.

Butch McGuire's 20 W. Division; 337-9080. Friendly, crowded singles bar.

Clark Street Cafe 2260 N. Clark; 549-4037. Bar section popular with singles crowd.

Emerald Isle Pub 21 E. Pearson; 944-9030. Irish pub.

Figaro's 7 E. Oak; 944-4440. Near North favorite; juke box plays jazz.

O'Rourke's Pub 319 W. North Avenue; 944-1030. Popular with artists and writers. Loud and rowdy on Friday nights.

Riccardo's 437 N. Rush; 787-2874. Friday nights this bar is wall to wall with writers, local TV personalities, and the advertising crowd. Closed weekends.

She-nannigans 16 W. Division; 642-2344. Singles and businessmen.

Sherlock's Home 900 N. Michigan; 787-0545. Like a London pub.

Toulouse 49 W. Division; 944-2606. Classy piano bar within a restaurant.

2350 Pub 2249 N. Lincoln Avenue; 281-9859. Popular neighborhood bar and restaurant.

Zanies 1548 N. Wells; 337-4027. Comedy nightclub/bar offers long-running Chicago satirical revue.

BASEBALL

See SPORTS.

BASKETBALL

See SPORTS.

BEAUTY SHOPS AND BARBERS

Black Hair Is 43 E. Oak; 787-0041.

Charles Ifergan 106 E. Oak; 642-4454. Cutting edge of chic; makeup lessons.

Colin of London 49 E. Oak; 664-8690. Men only.

Elizabeth Arden 717 N. Michigan; 266-5750. Body and beauty salon for women.

Gayle Johnson 46 E. Oak; 642-8395. Great haircuts for men and women.
Georgette Klinger Water Tower Place, 835 N. Michigan; 787-4300. Skin care; facials and massages.
Vidal Sassoon Water Tower Place, 835 N. Michigan; 751-2216. Complete hair care. Free haircuts given some weeknights for hairdresser practice.

BED AND BREAKFAST

For a European-style change of pace, stay with a family rather than in a hotel—**Bed and Breakfast Chicago**, 951-0085, can find the right accommodations with advance notice.

BICYCLES

See RENTALS.

BOOKS ABOUT CHICAGO

Guides and Histories

Best Restaurants of Chicago and Environs: A Revised and Greatly Expanded Edition by Sherman Kaplan. 101 Productions, 1979. Comprehensive guide.
The Business Traveler's Survival Guide: Chicago Business Travelers, Inc., 1981.
Chicago: A Historical Guide to the Neighborhoods 1830–1978 by Glen E. Holt and Dominic A. Pacyga. Chicago Historical Society, 1979.
The Chicago Art Review: The Art Explorer's Guide to Chicago by Leslie Krantz. The Krantz Co., 1979.

Chicago: Growth of a Metropolis by Harold M. Mayer and Richard C. Wade. University of Chicago Press, 1973. A historical study.

Chicago on Foot: An Architectural Walking Guide by Ira J. Bach. Rand McNally Publishing Co., 1977.

Chicago's Famous Buildings edited by Ira J. Bach. University of Chicago Press, 1980. An architectural guide.

Chicago Magazine's Guide to Chicago by Kelson-Spiselman-Novick-Klimovich. Contemporary Books, 1983.

Dr. Night Life's Chicago by Rick Kogan. Chicago Review Press, 1979. Pubs, nightclubs, discos.

500 Things to Do in Chicago for Free by Jim Hargrove and Patrick K. Snook. Follett Publishing Co., 1980.

The Lake is Always East by Caro, Gerbie, and Telingator. Follett Publishing Co., 1981. City guide.

Shopwatch by Laurie Levy. Chicago Review Press, 1980. Shopping and services.

Yesterday's Chicago by Herman Kogan and Rick Kogan. E. A. Seemann Press, 1976.

Books Set In Chicago

Boss, by Mike Royko.
The Jungle, by Upton Sinclair.
The Man with the Golden Arm, by Nelson Algren.
Sister Carrie, by Theodore Dreiser.
Studs Lonigan, by James Farrell.

BOOKSTORES

Abraham Lincoln Book Shop 18 E. Chestnut; 944-3085. Specializes in American history—politics, first editions, and autographs.

Barbara's Bookstore 1434 N. Wells; 642-5044. Also, 2907 N. Broadway; 477-0411. Emphasis on small presses, literature, the off-beat. Gives discount on New York *Times* Best Seller list books. Broadway store has performing arts annex.

CIVIL CENTER WITH SCULPTURE BY PICASSO

B. Dalton 175 W. Jackson; 922-5219. Merchandise Mart Plaza; 527-1370. 700 N. Michigan Avenue; 943-6872; 129 N. Wabash; 236-7615. They claim if they don't have it, probably no one does. Strong in popular titles.

China Books & Periodicals 174 W. Randolph; 782-6004. From mainland China; books, periodicals, and art-work.

Europa Book Store 3229 N. Clark; 929-1836. Foreign language books, periodicals, records.

Guild Books 2456 N. Lincoln; 525-3667. Thoughtful selection of fiction and nonfiction, poetry, foreign and domestic magazines; frequent appearances by such authors as Studs Terkel, Gwendolyn Brooks, Kurt Vonnegut, Jr.

Jewish Book Mart of Chicago 127 N. Dearborn, 2nd floor; 782-5199. New, used, and rare books in Hebrew and English.

Kroch's & Brentano's, Inc. 29 S. Wabash; 332-7500. 16 S. LaSalle; 332-7528. 516 N. Michigan; 321-0989. Water Tower Place; 943-2452. The large Wabash store is strong in art, business, and professional titles; other branches are smaller, with varying selections. Big gift departments, too.

Kroch's & Brentano's Bargain Book Center 62 E. Randolph; 263-2681. Remainders and close-outs.

Moody Bookstores 150 W. Chicago; 329-4352. 26 E. Adams; 346-2532. Christian readings, bibles, greeting cards. Large music section.

Oak Street Bookshop 54 E. Oak; 642-3070. A large theater and film section, plus a good selection of Chicago writers.

Occult Bookstore 3230 N. Clark; 281-0599. All subjects, including witchcraft, tarot, alchemy, yoga, psychic readings.

Rand McNally & Co. Bookstore 23 E. Madison; 267-6868. Maps and guidebooks.

Regency Book Shop 200 S. State, 7th floor; 786-9786. Usually 25 percent off best sellers and art books. Deliveries to Loop addresses.

Rizzoli International Bookstore Water Tower Place, 835 N. Michigan; 642-3500. High-quality store, with outstanding selections in art, music, architecture, and foreign language. Also, newsstand with rare publications and a large record section. Open late every night.

St. Paul Catholic Book Center 172 N. Michigan; 346-4228. Religious books, posters, cards.

Stuart Brent 670 N. Michigan; 337-6357. Emphasis on art, literature, travel, and psychiatric textbooks. Big children's section.

Timbuktu Books 2530 S. Michigan; 842-8242. Specializes in black literature.

Waldenbooks Sears Tower; 876-0308. 200 E. Randolph; 565-2489. Best sellers and popular interest.

Walton Books 172 E. Walton; 787-7635. "Dial-a-book" service to major Chicago hotels.

Women & Children First 1967 N. Halsted; 440-8824. Feminist center with books, stationery, and music. Large children's section.

Used Books

Aspidistra Bookshop 2630 N. Clark; 549-3129. No textbooks. Heavy on literature, biography, popular culture. Some first editions.

Booksellers Row 2445 N. Lincoln; 348-1170. Vast selection of hard-to-find titles, in good condition.

O'Gara's Bookstore 1311 E. 57th; 363-0993. Collectors' items and rare bindings mingle with used best sellers. Open until 10 P.M. every night.

Powell's Book Shop 1501 E. 57th; 955-7780. Rare and out-of-print books, plus lots of paperbacks and textbooks. Open until 11 P.M. every night.

BOUTIQUES

Ann Taylor 103 E. Oak; 943-5411. Favorite place for young, sophisticated crowd. Sportswear and shoes are strong departments.

Apropos 3315 N. Broadway; 528-2130. Fantastic selection of sweaters, lingerie, socks, and accessories. Lots of silk blouses, separates, and Danskins.

Barbara Weed 66 E. Walton; 944-1218. Emphasis on chic European sportswear.

Bottega Glaseia 106 E. Oak; 337-0777. Quality fashions imported from Paris and Milan.

Brittany, Ltd. 642 N. Michigan; 642-6550. Classic tailored separates: Ralph Lauren, Burberry, J. G. Hook. Great blazers and suits; free alterations for women.

Burberry's 633 N. Michigan; 787-2500. That certain look—imported from England. Famous trench coats, sweaters, woolens; trademark plaid accessories.

Caché Water Tower Place, 835 N. Michigan; 951-8230. Well known for its extravagant evening fashions; designer sportswear, too.

Dana Cote D'azur Water Tower Place, 835 N. Michigan; 787-8611. Classic French sportswear.

Degagé, Inc. 2252 N. Clark; 935-7737. A sophisticated mix of the trendy and traditional; everything a little unusual.

Laura Ashley Water Tower Place, 835 N. Michigan; 951-8004. Victorian England—lace, tiny prints, ruffles—reinterpreted in modern-day dress.

Luv Boutique 2106–10 N. Clark; 929-2330. Sportswear, silks, and suits by D. D. Dominick, Paul Stanley, and others. Extensive beachwear collection; career women's corner.

Merchant of Venice 2260 N. Lincoln; 477-5005. Trendy and unique women's sportswear.

MW Career Dress Off Center, 300 W. Grand; 661-1094. Everything you need to dress for success—at a discount.

My Sister's Circus 101 E. Oak; 664-7074. Trend-setting clothes in fun atmosphere; wide selection of swimwear in the "Bikini Zoo."

Nonpareil 2300 N. Clark; 477-2933. Contemporary women's wear with the emphasis on novelty, quality, and the chic, offbeat.

Polo Ralph Lauren 906 N. Michigan; 280-0550. Everything by the American Westernwear Master, Lauren himself.

Pompian Shop 57 E. Oak; 337-6604. Quality fashions; great sportswear.

Port of Entry 2032 N. Halsted; 348-4550. One-of-a-kind trend setters.

Presence 2534 N. Clark; 248-1761. Danskins and casual fashions; some nice vintage pieces. Reasonably priced.

Quintessence Water Tower Place, 835 N. Michigan; 944-7781. Very chic and kicky.

Stanley Korshak 940 N. Michigan; 280-0520. Quality clothes in separate boutiques; big names, chic designs, expensive prices.

Sugar Magnolia 110 E. Oak; 944-0885. Very up-to-the-minute fashions and accessories, with lots of punk surprises.

Therese, Inc. 70 E. Oak; 951-0410. Chic fashions, including ultra suedes of Halstons, for sizes 14 through 26.

Ultimo 114 E. Oak; 787-0906. Trend-setting clothes from Europe and top young designers. High, high fashion for high prices.

BUSES

See TRANSPORTATION.

CAR RENTALS

See TRANSPORTATION.

CERAMICS, CHINA, GLASS, AND POTTERY

Crate & Barrel 850 N. Michigan; 787-5900. The best of the moderns.

Crystal Suite Water Tower Place, 835 N. Michigan; 944-1320. Baccarat, Kosta Boda, Lalique, and other famous names in this elegant shop.

Distinctive Interior Designs 2322 N. Clark; 248-0738. This store is almost unbeatable for its exquisite taste and friendly service. Special orders taken. Closed Mondays.

Lill Street Potters 1021 W. Lill; 477-0701. Innovative stoneware and porcelains.

Spaulding & Co. 959 N. Michigan; 337-4800. This 100-year-old store carries the finest quality china, crystal, and its own hallmark silver.

Tiffany & Co. 715 N. Michigan; 944-7500.

CHEESE SHOPS

See also GOURMET FOODS.

Chalet Wine & Cheese Shop 444 W. Fullerton; 871-0300. Also, 405 W. Armitage; 266-7155, and 3000 N. Clark; 935-9400. Hundreds of imported and domestic cheeses.

CHILDREN AND CHILDREN'S THINGS

Clothes

Born Beautiful 3206 N. Broadway; 549-6770.
City Child 2413 N. Lincoln; 935-0266. The chicest children dress here.
Clown 72 E. Oak; 642-6636. Imported and whimsical clothes; designer quality.
Lady Madonna Maternity Boutique Water Tower Place, 835 N. Michigan; 266-2420. Layettes to toddlers.
Merchant of Venice 2260 N. Lincoln; 477-5005. Fashionable and one-of-a-kind duds.
Over the Rainbow Water Tower Place, 835 N. Michigan; 943-2050. Great selection of beautiful dress outfits and stylish, rugged everyday wear.
Pam's Young Folks Water Tower Place, 835 N. Michigan; 951-0292. Designer names for kids.

Day Care

If you're staying in a hotel, the management or concierge can probably make arrangements for you. Also call:
American Registry for Nurses & Sitters 348-8514. Closed Saturdays and Sundays.
Chicago Parents Club 878-4270.

FIELD MUSEUM OF NATURAL HISTORY

Entertainment

Check the "Kid Stuff" listings in *Chicago* magazine.

Museums

See MUSEUMS for complete information.

Chicago Historical Society North Avenue at Clark; 642-4600. Special demonstrations of pioneer skills.
Field Museum of Natural History 1400 S. Lake Shore; 922-9410. Kids love the Hall of Dinosaurs, mummies, and the African Watering Hole.
Junior Museum Art Institute Michigan Avenue at Adams; 443-3500. Also has a special Junior Gift Shop.
Museum of Science and Industry 57th and Lake Shore Drive; 684-1414. Especially for the young and young-at-heart, this is a participatory museum: you can push buttons, turn cranks, go through a coal mine or German submarine. Also, a spectacular fairy dollhouse.

Playgrounds and Parks

Lincoln Park playground 2300 N. in the park. Equipped playground just north of the zoo.

Supervised by the Chicago Park District, a number of beaches line the lakefront. Major ones include: Oak Street to Ohio Street, 500 to 1000 N.; North Avenue, 1600 N.; and Fullerton Avenue, 2400 N.

See also TOYS AND ZOOS.

CHOCOLATE AND CANDY

Aunt Diana's Old-Fashioned Fudge Water Tower Place, 845 N. Michigan; 664-1535. Nine different flavors.

Fannie May Shops 433 N. Michigan; 751-8517. Also, 51 E. Randolph; 263-8291, and 12 S. LaSalle; 263-8134.

Godiva Chocolates Water Tower Place, 835 N. Michigan; 280-1133.

Krön Chocolatier Water Tower Place, 835 N. Michigan; 943-8444. Hand-dipped strawberries. Chocolate novelties. Open very late.

Long Grove Confectionary Co. 140 E. Walton; 642-1684.

Marshall Field & Co. 111 N. State; 781-1000. Huge first-floor candy dept.

Martha's Candy Shop 3257 N. Broadway; 248-8733. Fresh candy made daily. Personalized service.

CHURCHES
See SIGHTS WORTH SEEING.

COFFEE AND TEA
See also GOURMET FOODS.

Coffee & Tea Exchange 3300 N. Broadway; 528-2241.
Coffee Corner 1700 N. Wells; 951-7638.
Cook's Mart 609 N. LaSalle; 642-3526. Also, Water Tower Place, 845 N. Michigan; 280-0929.
Something's Brewing 2828 N. Clark (Century Shopping Center, 6th level); 871-7475. Custom blends, accouterments, tiny café in back with stunning pastries.

CONCERTS
See MUSIC.

COSMETICS

Boyd's Chemists 940 N. Michigan; 280-0520. Inside the Stanley Korshak boutique.
Georgette Klinger, Inc. Water Tower Place, 835 N. Michigan; 787-4300. Skin-care products and makeup.
Marilyn Miglin Model Makeup 112 E. Oak; 943-1120.

DANCE

Between local repertory groups and recognized traveling companies, Chicago's dance scene is always hopping. The theater arts sections of the 2 daily papers carry notices; the most complete listings can be found in Sections One and Two of the *Reader*, a free weekly paper available on Fridays at many book and record stores, and some restaurants. Also, check *Chicago* magazine.

Also, the Chicago Council on the Arts answers questions on artistic performances. Call F-I-N-E-A-R-T or 346-3278.

Tickets

Hot Tix Booth Daley Center Plaza, Dearborn and Randolph; 977-1755. On the day of performance, Hot Tix offers tickets at half price. Hours are Tuesday–Thursday, 11 A.M.–6 P.M.; Saturday, 10 A.M.–5 P.M. Pick up tickets for Sunday and Monday performances on Saturday.
Ticketron Ticket service agency. Dial T-I-C-K-E-T-S or 842-5387, for a recording about all performances covered by Ticketron. Monday–Friday, call 454-6777 for information on ticket availability.

Companies

Chicago Contemporary Dance Theatre 2257 N. Lincoln; 643-8916.

Chicago Moving Company 2433 N. Lincoln; 929-7416. Modern dance.

Joel Hall Dancers 410 S. Michigan; 663-3618. Favorite local jazz troupe.

Joseph Holmes Dance Theater 3206 N. Wilton; 975-3505. Black dance group.

Lou Conte's Hubbard St. Dance Company 218 S. Wabash; 461-0892. Specializing in jazz.

MoMing Dance & Arts Center 1034 W. Barry; 472-9894. Home for the unusual and the avant-garde.

Lessons

Chicago Dance Center 2433 N. Lincoln; 929-7416. Offers classes in ballet, modern, jazz. Special children's classes.

Gus Giordano Dance Center 614 Davis, Evanston; 866-9442. Well-known for classes in jazz and modern dance.

Ida Borchard & The Modern Dance Center 410 S. Michigan; 427-0789. Classes taught in the mode of Mary Wigman and Isadora Duncan.

DAY CARE

See CHILDREN AND CHILDREN'S THINGS.

DENTISTS

See HOSPITALS AND HEALTH EMERGENCIES.

DEPARTMENT STORES

Bonwit Teller 875 N. Michigan; 751-8000. Located on the ground floor of the John Hancock Building, Bonwit's has a large perfume section, a Hermès shop with leather goods and scarves, and fashions for men and women.

Carson Pirie Scott & Co. 1 S. State; 744-2000. The beautiful Louis Sullivan façade was recently restored to its former glory; now it's a Chicago landmark. Special attractions include the model rooms on the 5th floor and Kitchen-tech—a complete demonstration kitchen—on the 7th. Every fall, Carson's produces an elaborate "Import Fair" with goods from foreign countries. The Personal/Telephone Shopping Service number is 372-6800. Carson charge cards only.

Chas. A. Stevens 25 N. State; 630-1500. Also, Water Tower Place, 845 N. Michigan. Women's fashions and accessories. Known for its designer boutiques and well-stocked shoe department, Stevens also has a career woman's department called "Executive Place."

I. Magnin & Co. 830 N. Michigan; 751-0500. Just like its San Francisco sister, this store gets high marks for quality and chic styling. Famous for carrying designer lines; lots of Yves St. Laurent and Cartier. I. Magnin and American Express cards only.

Lane Bryant 9 N. Wabash; 621-8700. Department store for the hard-to-fit woman, teenager, and little girl.

Lord & Taylor Water Tower Place, 835 N. Michigan; 787-7400. Well-stocked in sportswear and accessories.

Marshall Field & Co. 111 N. State; 781-1000. Also, Water Tower Place, 835 N. Michigan. Started in 1852 as a dry-goods store, Fields is a Chicago institution today. Most Chicagoans feel if you can't find it there, it's not worth having. The newly refinished State Street is the most complete—with a vast toy department, encompassing book department, china and crystal rooms, antiques, and a confectionary department with candy fresh from Fields' own kitchens. A must is the famous Frango Mint. Also, try the restaurants—including the English Room, Walnut Room (packed during Christmas), and the Crystal Palace Ice Cream Parlor. Fields' and American Express credit cards.

Neiman-Marcus 737 N. Michigan; 642-5900. All the glamour and glitz of the Texas store. A superb gourmet shop, the latest oversized fashions from France and Japan, and two fantastic shoe departments. Plus a nice surprise: not everything costs the moon—it just looks like it does.

Saks Fifth Avenue 669 N. Michigan; 944-6500. Equivalent of the New York City store with top-line fashions and accessories. This store has an expanded men's department and a busy beauty salon. Sales, when they occur, offer tremendous bargains.

DISCOS

See NIGHTLIFE.

DRUGSTORES

Walgreens 1130 N. State; 787-6633. This drugstore (plus liquor store) has the latest hours in the Loop and Near North areas: 8 A.M.–2 A.M. MasterCard and Visa acceptable.

If you need a prescription at 2 A.M., call **Parkway Drugs**, 2368 N. Clark; 549-2720. Open 24 hours, they'll accept Visa or MasterCard (no American Express) and deliver to your door.

ETHNIC NEIGHBORHOODS AND SHOPS

Chinatown 22nd & Wentworth. Two-block shopping district: restaurants, grocery stores, gift shops.
German Community 4000 to 4400 blocks of N. Lincoln.
Greek Town 100 to 300 blocks of S. Halsted.
Little Italy 900–1200 W. Taylor. Restaurants, grocery stores, residential rehabs of turn-of-the-century buildings on side streets to the north.
Polish Community 1200 to 2200 blocks of N. Milwaukee. Restaurants, bookstores, daily Polish newspaper available.

See also RESTAURANTS.

Specialty Shops

Acropolis Gift Shop 306 S. Halsted; 332-1182. Greek imports, including lots of tavli sets.

Arirang 3330 N. Clark; 929-7900. Korean grocery.

Chinese Books & Periodicals 174 W. Randolph; 782-6004.

Conte Di Savoia 555 W. Roosevelt; 666-3471. Italian grocery.

Cuban Boy's Spanish Book 1225 W. 18th; 243-5911. Cuban books, newspapers, magazines.

Erinisle 1959 N. Halsted; 280-0082. Beautiful knits and tweeds, tableware, designer sportswear, pottery, and crystal.

F. Pancner, Importer 6514 W. Cermak Rd., Berwyn; 484-3459. Czech books, records, dolls, greeting cards, and gifts.

Framo Publishers/Lyra Books 561 W. Diversey; 477-1484. Hungarian bookstore.

Gifts International 2501 W. 71st; 471-1424. Lithuanian gifts and books.

Happy Garden Bakery 2358 S. Wentworth; 225-2730. Chinese bakery.

Hellas Pastry 2627 W. Lawrence; 271-7500. Great baklava and saraglie.

Indian Tree 233 E. Ontario; 642-1607. Antique and contemporary American Indian paintings, bead work, pottery.

Japan Books & Records 3347 N. Clark; 248-4114.

Kiyo's 2831 N. Clark; 935-0619. Classy Japanese gift shop.

Kuhn's 3051 N. Lincoln; 525-9019. German delicatessen and grocery with lots of European specialties; for many, Christmas isn't Christmas without a visit.

Leonard's Bakery 2651 W. Devon; 743-0318. Bagels, challah, sour-cream sweet rolls.

Lutz Continental Cafe 2458 W. Montrose; 478-7785. Fantastic, well-known bakery-café.

Mexican Folk Arts 2433 N. Clark; 871-1511. Quality items, including sweaters, pottery, and blankets.

Mexican Shop 801 Dempster St., Evanston; 475-8665. Large store with lots of interesting items—clothes, pottery, furniture, jewelry.

Omiyage Ltd. 2482 N. Lincoln; 477-1428. Japanese gift shop; some antiques, very clever and trendy items.

Polonia Bookstore 2886 N. Milwaukee; 489-2554. Largest Polish bookstore in U.S.

Sajewski Music Store 1227 N. Milwaukee; 276-3452. Polish music center.

Scandinavian Design 920 N. Michigan; 664-9232. China, textiles, silver.

Schmid Imports 4606 N. Lincoln; 561-2871. German gifts: clocks, pipes, china, books.

Schwartz-Rosenblum 2906 W. Devon; 338-3919. Hebrew bookstore.

Shamrock Imports 3150 N. Laramie; 286-6866. Irish music—contemporary and traditional.

Supermercado Maria Cardenos 1758 W. 18th; 733-9649. Hispanic grocery.

Timbuktu 2530 S. Michigan; 842-8242. Books by and about blacks.

Tomas Bakery 4054 N. Lincoln; 472-6401. Delicious Serbo-Croatian delicacies.

Vesecky's Bakery 6634 W. Cermak Road, Berwyn; 788-4144. Czech specialties.

Wah Leung Hong 2416 S. Wentworth; 225-8303. A Chinese herbal drugstore.

Wah May 2403 S. Wentworth; 225-2730. Chinese grocery.

Wikstrom Gourmet Foods 5247 N. Clark; 878-0601. Everything you need for a Scandinavian smorgasbord.

EXCURSIONS OUT OF THE CITY

Cantigny 151 Winfield Road, Wheaton; 668-5161. The 500-acre estate of the late Robert McCormick, publisher of the *Tribune*. Sights include a 10-acre formal garden and 2 museums: one the Georgian McCormick mansion, another dedicated to military memorabilia. Picnic grounds also. The estate grounds are open daily 9 A.M.–7 P.M.; military museum 9 A.M.–5 P.M.; the mansion is open Wednesday–Sunday, 12–4 P.M. Admission free.

Galena An overnight trip to a charming town on the Mississippi River. An antique shoppers delight, with dozens of stores. The beautifully restored home of Ulysses S. Grant is there; so is the balcony where Lincoln and Douglas debated. Don't come without a motel reservation; Galena is often booked up. Car trip recommended; Greyhound service. 164 miles.

Indiana Dunes State Park This is a federally proclaimed National Lakeshore with swimming, hiking, and camping opportunities. Reached by car or South Shore Railroad Line. 40 miles.

Lake Geneva, Wisconsin Popular resort area, with luxury hotels or adequate motels. Lake fishing, sailing, swimming; parks with horseback riding. Skiing, ice fishing, and snowmobiling in winter. Reached by car, Greyhound, or Chicago Northwestern Railroad. 75 miles.

FABRIC SHOPS

Clothworks Water Tower Place, 835 N. Michigan; 266-0282. Bold modern graphics.

Crate & Barrel 850 N. Michigan; 787-5900. Extensive collection of Marimekko fabrics.

Laura Ashley Water Tower Place, 835 N. Michigan; 951-8004. Stylish little prints from England.

Pierre Deux 113 E. Oak; 642-9657. French provincial prints.

Vogue Fabrics 718 Main Street, Evanston; 864-9600; also, Water Tower Place, 835 N. Michigan; 787-2521. Good prices, super selection of everything from seersucker to designer silks.

FISHING BOATS AND EQUIPMENT

See RENTALS.

FOOTBALL

See SPORTS.

FURS

North Beach Leather Water Tower Place, 835 N. Michigan; 280-9292. Fox, coyote, sheepskin.
Thomas E. McElroy Furs 717 N. Michigan; 943-7878.
Thorpe Furs Water Tower Place, 845 N. Michigan; 337-1750.

GAY SCENE

Neighborhoods

Although gays and their activities can be found anywhere in the city, there are 2 chief neighborhoods considered part of "the community." New Town runs from the corner of Diversey-Broadway-Clark north to Belmont-Broadway. Then there's the area a few blocks west of the down-town Near North section—especially the 400 to 700 blocks of Clark and Dearborn, plus the side streets of Illinois and Hubbard. During the summer, gay sections of the Lake Michigan beach can be found at the Oak Street beach and, farther north, at the Belmont Rocks, a stretch of sand between Wellington and Belmont.

Information

Gay Life 951-8300. A free weekly paper with complete, up-to-date listings.

Men's Bars

Annex 2 430 N. Clark; 644-5268. Lots of dancing; some leather.
Big Red's 3019 N. Clark; 525-1200.
BJ's 3231 N. Clark; 477-3404.
Bushes 3320 N. Halsted; 525-6088. Fast action.
Carol's Speakeasy 1355 N. Wells; 944-4226. An easy-going crowd and lots of parties.
Cheeks 2730 N. Clark; 348-3400. With one of the latest closings, this bar is very wild and rowdy.
Dandy's 2632 N. Halsted; 975-6373. Piano bar.
Foster's 4086 N. Broadway; 929-6070.
Glory Hole 1343 N. Wells; 944-9065. Hot and heavy.
Gold Coast 5025 N. Clark; 878-5970. Very leather and Levi's
Inner Circle 2546 N. Clark; 880-5511.
Kitty Sheon 906 Ernst Ct; 944-9646. Traditional crowd.
Little Jim's 3501 N. Halsted; 871-6116. Friendly place that's open early in the day.
Loading Zone 46 E. Oak; 266-2244. Disco with lots of action.
Manhandler 1948 N. Halsted; 871-3339. Lots of leather.
New Flight 420 N. Clark; 467-5551. Popular with party crowd.
Sam's 2540 N. Clark; 477-0299.
Touche 2825 N. Lincoln; 929-3269. Heavily into leather and Levi's.

Baths

All gay baths in Chicago are operated as private membership clubs. Memberships are usually available but not always at the door. Call ahead for details.

Club Chicago 609 N. LaSalle; 337-0080.
Man's Country 5015 N. Clark; 878-2069.
Unicorn Club 3246 N. Halsted; 929-6080.

Women's Bars

Augie's/C.K.'s 3726 N. Broadway; 975-0449. Friendly place.

Lady Bug 3445 N. Halsted; 281-3336.
Swan Club 3720 N. Clark; 327-4884.

Mixed Bars

Baton Show Lounge 436 N. Clark; 644-5269. Female impersonators.
Closet 3325 N. Broadway; 477-8533. Friendly neighborhood bar.
La Cage Chicago 50 E. Oak; 944-3300. Elaborate disco drag show club.

Bookstores

Locker 53 W. Hubbard; 923-9210.
Machine Shop 504 N. Clark; 337-9098.
Ram 3511½ N. Halsted; 525-9528.

The following general interest bookstores have large gay sections:

Barbara's Bookstore 1434 N. Wells; 642-5044. 2907 N. Broadway; 477-0411.
Unabridged Books 3251 N. Broadway; 883-9119.
Women & Children First 1967 N. Halsted; 440-8824.

Restaurants

These restaurants cater to both a gay and straight clientele:

Ann Sather 925 W. Belmont; 348-2378.
Belden Corned Beef Center 2315 N. Clark; 935-2752.
Hippo 50 E. Oak; 944-3300.
Medinah 2401 N. Clark; 929-3030.
My Brother's Place 111 W. Hubbard; 321-0776.
Ricky's 3181 N. Broadway; 549-3136.

Counseling/Hotline

AIDS Hotline 871-5696.
Chicago Men's Gathering 561-8814. Discussion group for married/bisexual men.
Chicagoland Youthhelp, Inc. 337-2424.
Gay Horizons 929-HELP. Hotline open from 7–11 P.M.

Gender Services 472-4518. Group for transvestites, transsexuals.
Howard Brown Memorial Clinic 2676 N. Halsted; 871-5777. Medical testing and treatment.
In Touch Hotline 996-5535. Youth counseling.
Lesbian Community Center 3435 N. Sheffield; 549-4370. This drop-in center for women and children, Monday–Friday, 6–10 P.M.; Saturday, 2–6 P.M.
Mattachine Midwest 337-2424.
Metro-Help 929-8907. Hotline.
National Coalition of Black Gays 236-0764.
Review 620-6946. Group for bi and gay married men.
Talkline 228-6400. 24-hour hotline.
Women In Crisis Can Act 528-3303.

Political Groups

Gay & Lesbian Coalition of Metropolitan Chicago 764-2024.
Illinois Gay & Lesbian Task Force 975-0707.
Organization to Promote Equality Now 236-0803.

Religious Services

Congregation Or Chadash 656 W. Barry; 248-9456. Jewish services every second and fourth Friday at 8:30 P.M.
Dignity/Chicago 824 W. Wellington; 549-2633. Catholic services at 7 P.M. Sunday.
Good Shepherd Parish 615 W. Wellington; 472-8708. Nondenominational Christian services every Sunday at 7 P.M.

Social and Cultural Groups

Artemis Singers 267-8972. Lesbian chorus group.
Black & White Men Together 472-4865.
Chicago Gay/Lesbian Community Band 878-8980.
Gay Athletic Association 447-4349.
Maturity 372-8616. Monthly meetings for those over 40.
Professionals Over 30 929-7666.
Speak Its Name 565-2278. Performing arts group.
Toddlin' Town Performing Arts 248-6929.
Windy City Athletic Association 525-3398.

Windy City Gay Chorus 227-3853.
Windy City Wrestling Club 525-7608.

Events
Gay Pride Week and Annual Parade A full week of activities takes place in June. For details, call the Gay/Lesbian Pride Planning Committee, 348-8243.

GOURMET FOODS

Chalet Wine & Cheese Shops 444 W. Fullerton; 871-0300. 405 W. Armitage; 266-7155. Extensive selection of wine, cheese, bread, and cheese cakes.
City Market at the Century 2828 N. Clark; 525-9072. From vichyssoise to pignoli, fresh, fashionable foods.
Kenessey 403 W. Belmont; 929-7500. Eat in the intimate café or take out selections from the pastry shop; also superb sausages and cheeses. Over 1,500 different wines. Will make up gourmet picnic baskets.
LaSalle Street Market 745 N. LaSalle; 943-7450. Gourmet deli.
Mitchell Cobey Cuisine 100 E. Walton; 944-3411. Quality take-out, including quiches, cheese cakes, pâtés, salads. Also does catering.
Pfaelzer Brothers 4501 W. District Boulevard; 927-7100. Gourmet meats (steaks the specialty) shipped anywhere. Orders by phone; credit cards taken.
Treasure Island 1639 N. Wells; 642-1105. Also, 75 E. Elm; 440-1144. "The Gourmet Supermarket."

GYMS AND INDOOR SPORTS FACILITIES

Many hotels have guest arrangements with health clubs and gyms. Also, some health/sports clubs will charge a 1- or 2-day guest fee for out-of-towners.

Chicago Health & Tennis Clubs 300 N. State; 321-9600. 230 W. Monroe 263-4500.

East Bank Club 500 N. Kingsbury; 527-5800.

Illinois Center Racquet Club 111 E. Wacker; 861-1220.

McClurg Court Sports Center 333 E. Ontario; 944-4546.

Mid-Town Tennis Club 2020 W. Fullerton; 235-2300.

Riviera 400 Health Club 400 E. Randolph; 527-2525.

YMCA 30 W. Chicago; 944-6211. Offers a daily membership pass ($8.50 for men, $6 for women) that covers use of the pool, gym, weight room, steam, and sauna. An additional fee covers handball, racquetball, and squash courts.

HABERDASHERIES

Bigsby & Kruthers Water Tower Place, 835 N. Michigan; 944-6955. Also, 205 W. Monroe; 236-6633. They call themselves "The Suit People." Designers YSL, Blass, Klein, Missoni ties; Special Men Under 5'8" Shop.

Brittany, Ltd. 642 N. Michigan; 642-6550. Also, 29 S. LaSalle; 372-5985. Fashionable haberdashers; Ralph Lauren, Izod, Burberry.

Britts 646 N. Michigan; 642-7888. Supposedly the "bargain basement" of Brittany, Ltd., but often identical items can be found here for less bucks.

Brooks Brothers 74 E. Madison; 263-0100. Traditional and conservative suits, sportscoats, separates.

Burberry's 633 N. Michigan; 787-2500. That certain look—imported from England. Famous trench coats, sweaters, woolens, jackets; trademark plaid accessories.

Capper & Capper 1 N. Wabash; 236-3800. Also, 909 N. Michigan; 236-3800. Conservatively elegant menswear.

Dana Côte D'Azur Water Tower Place, 835 N. Michigan; 787-8611. French designer clothes.

Davis for Men 41 E. Oak; 751-2582.

Gentry Shop Water Tower Place, 835 N. Michigan; 337-2650. Names like Hart Schaffner and Marx and Hickey-Freeman.

Hart Schaffner & Marx Clothing 36 S. Franklin; 372-6300.

M. Hyman and Son Water Tower Place, 835 N. Michigan; 266-0060. Big and tall sizes for hard-to-fit men.

Mark Shale 919 N. Michigan; 440-0720. Great selection of suits, sweaters, and outdoors wear.

Marks Ltd. 2756 N. Racine; 883-4477. Designer clothes "for the shorter man."

Morry's Men's Wear 645 N. Michigan; 642-1610.

Polo Ralph Lauren 906 N. Michigan; 280-0550.

HOCKEY

See SPORTS.

HOSPITALS AND HEALTH EMERGENCIES

Hospitals

All of these hospital emergency rooms are only a 5- to 10-minute car ride within the Near North/downtown area. In an emergency, call 911 for a city ambulance, which will take you to the nearest emergency room.

Augustana Hospital & Health Care Center 411 W. Dickens; 975-5000. No credit cards accepted.

Grant Hospital 551 W. Grant; 883-2000. Operates trauma and alcoholism units. No credit cards.

Henrotin Hospital 111 W. Oak; 440-7700. Visa cards acceptable.

Northwestern Memorial Hospital Superior & Fairbanks; 649-2000. This hospital has a large staff and selection of services, plus 1,000 beds. Takes American Express, Visa, and MasterCard in emergency room.

Dental Referral

Chicago Dental Society 726-4076, 726-4321. Free referral line operates Monday–Friday, 9 A.M.–5 P.M.

Medical Referral

Augustana Hospital 975-5243. The "Doctor Is In" program operates around the clock. Just call and you'll get an appointment within 24–72 hours, with the appropriate physician.

Contact Lens Repair

Boll & Lewis 111 N. Wabash #1812; 782-5709. Also, 645 N. Michigan; 266-0520. Offers 1-day emergency service.

HOTELS

You shouldn't come to Chicago without a hotel reservation; this is a convention town, which means that all too often, everything is booked to the rafters. If you do risk it, however, the Greater Chicago Hotel and Motel Association can give you an availability report on local rooms. Call 236-3473, Monday–Friday, during business hours.

Almost every hotel has a safety deposit box for valuables; use it. Also, every hotel can assist you with transportation to the airport. Most places have parking accommodations for guests for a fee of $6 and up a day.

Chicago is known for its fine selection of small, elegant hotels on the Near North Side. Older, more conventional accommodations can be found downtown.

Almost every hotel offers a variety of special weekend packages, which usually include some meals and entertainment. Definitely call ahead for reservations for those.

Downtown

Americana Congress 520 S. Michigan; (312) 427-3800, (800) 621-4404. Newly renovated hotel that is popular with business travelers. Some rooms have a view of lake. Prices start at $75.

THE WATER TOWER AND NORTH MICHIGAN AVENUE

Conrad Hilton 720 S. Michigan; (312) 922-4400, (800) 325-4620. Largest hotel in the city (2,279 rooms), this hotel is popular with conventions. Standardized, ample rooms. Not many services. Prices start at $80 a day and up.

Executive House 71 E. Wacker Dr.; 346-7100. Smaller, low-keyed hotel. Very functional. Priced at $70 and up.

Hyatt Regency Chicago 151 E. Wacker Dr.; (312) 565-1000, (800) 228-9000. Big and bustling. Nicely appointed rooms; some extremely deluxe suites. Many amenities. Priced at $95 and up.

Midland Hotel 172 W. Adams; 332-1200. Small, low-keyed place. Close to financial district. Nice rooms with bath-dressing room combination. Few amenities. Prices start at $60.

Palmer House 17 E. Monroe; 726-7500. Old World elegance in lobby. Rooms pleasant though sometimes small. Prices start at $70.

Near North

Ambassador East 1301 N. State Parkway; (312) 787-7200, (800) 228-2121. Popular with celebrities, this hotel has a very classy atmosphere. Tight security. VIP executive services; rooms are expensively decorated. Other services available: 24-hour medical and dental aid on call, baby-sitters, foreign currency exchange. Guests have use of health club facilities nearby. Priced from $120 and up.

Ambassador West 1300 N. State Parkway; (312) 787-7900, (800) 621-8090. A little less expensive than its sister hotel, and also a little less glamorous. Lobby furnished in genuine British antiques. Rooms clean and large. Health and sports club facilities nearby. Kosher kitchen. Priced from $90 and up.

Barclay Chicago 166 E. Superior; (312) 787-6000, (800) 621-8004. Just off Michigan Avenue, this new little hotel offers a fantastic location for less-than-excessive prices. Many rooms have kitchens; 2 restaurants, 3 cocktail lounges, and conference facilities are available. One block from Water Tower Place. Priced from $85–$135.

Chicago Marriott Hotel 540 N. Michigan; (312) 836-0100, (800) 228-9290. Big hotel, often filled with conventioners. Its own health club. Complete services, including rental car and airline offices. Rooms are very small. Pets allowed. Prices start at $95.

Drake Hotel 140 E. Walton Place; (312) 787-2000, (800) 323-7500. A glorious old luxury hotel in peak condition. Rooms have big closets, high ceilings, spacious baths. Bed-sitting rooms available; suites with bars and refrigerators. Some beautiful views of lake. Concierge. Prices start at $95.

Holiday Inn City Centre 300 E. Ohio; (312) 787-6100, (800) 238-8000. Popular with business travelers. Free parking for guests. Health and sports club facilities available for a fee. Prices start at $65.

Holiday Inn Lake Shore Drive 644 N. Lake Shore Drive; (312) 943-9200, (800) 238-8000. Free garage. Great views of city or lake. Health and sports club available. Prices start at $65.

Holiday Inn Mart Plaza 350 N. Orleans; (312) 836-5000, (800) 238-8000. Close to Merchandise Mart and Apparel Center. Free parking. Affiliated with trendy East Bank Club for sports and health club. Prices start at $65.

Knickerbocker Chicago Walton Place at N. Michigan Avenue; (312) 751-8100, (800) 621-8140. Popular with Europeans. Newly renovated, big rooms—some with 2 baths. Some rooms specially outfitted for wheelchairs. Priced from $90 and up.

Mayfair Regent 181 E. Lake Shore Drive; (312) 787-8500, (800) 621-8135. A new, elegant small hotel. Fantastic views of lake and city. Unusual: changing rooms, with deluxe baths. Junior suites; concierge service. Pets allowed. Priced from $125 and up.

Park Hyatt 800 N. Michigan Avenue; (312) 280-2222, (800) 228-9000. Chicago's trendiest hotel. In the winter, the doormen wear mink coats. Expensive furnishings; salon-lobby. Full services with concierge. Rooms tend to be small; junior suites available. Multilingual staff. Priced from $110 and up.

Raphael 201 E. Delaware Place; (312) 943-5000, (800) 327-9157. Great location (near Water Tower Place), plus classic elegance at low prices. European flavor. Tight security. Every room has a refrigerator. Concierge staff. Prices start at $70.

Ritz-Carlton 160 E. Pearson Street; (312) 266-1000, (800) 621-6906. Tucked behind Water Tower Place, this hotel is pure luxury. Extremely good security.

Classy atmosphere. Rooms have good views, electric blankets, lockable closets. Duplex suites. Telex available. Also, in-hour dry-cleaning. Pool and whirlpool for guests. Prices start at $100.

Sheraton-Plaza Hotel 160 E. Huron; (312) 787-2900, (800) 325-3535. Good location, rooftop pool. Concierge service. Small pets allowed. Many rooms have king-sized beds, some kitchenettes. Prices start at $80.

Tremont 100 E. Chestnut; (312) 751-1900, (800) 621-8133. Another small, elegant hotel. Top-quality service; health club facilities available. Rooms small but tastefully appointed. Prices at $95 and up.

Westin Hotel North Michigan Avenue at Delaware; (312) 943-7200, (800) 228-3000. Currently finishing extensive renovation. Good security. One block from Water Tower Place. Concierge staff. Small pets allowed with advanced notice. Health club in hotel. Prices start at $85 to $100.

Whitehall 105 E. Delaware; (312) 944-6300, (800) 223-5757. Luxurious small hotel. Attentive concierge staff. Good security. Big, bright rooms. Pets allowed. Many amenities. Priced at $100 and up.

O'Hare

Hyatt Regency O'Hare (312) 696-1234, (800) 228-9000. More amenities than usual for an airport hotel. Nicely appointed rooms. Prices start at $85.

O'Hare Hilton (312) 686-8000. Connected to the airport by underground concourse. Prices start at $80 to $100.

HOUSEWARES AND COOKING UTENSILS

Most of the department stores—especially Marshall Field's and Carson Pirie Scott—have excellent houseware sections. Here's a look at the specialty stores:

Cook's Mart 609 N. LaSalle; 642-3526. Also, Water Tower Place, 835 N. Michigan; 280-0929. Le Creuset cookware plus lots of gadgets and a big bakery section. Many different lessons—including 1-day ones—are available; name cooks often put on demonstrations. Coffee, tea, spices, and cookbook departments.

Corrado Cutlery 26 N. Clark; 368-8450. Knives, scissors, electrical converters/adapters for foreign appliances.

Crate & Barrel 850 N. Michigan; 787-5900. Everything you need for ethnic cooking can be found here. Modern cookware, including Copco and Calphalon; also lots of copper. Bargains are downstairs.

Crate & Barrel Warehouse 1510 N. Wells; 787-4775. This store is devoted to seconds, odd lots, and closeouts—all in good condition and at low prices.

Kitchen Store 744 W. Fullerton; 472-1597. A small bakery section offers coffee, tea, and croissants for shoppers.

ICE SKATES

See RENTALS.

INFORMATION

Cultural Information Booth Daley Center, between Clark and Dearborn at Washington; 443-7984. Free guide book to Loop sculpture and free CTA map.

Information Center 800 N. Michigan (inside the old Water Tower).

State Street Council 36 S. State; 782-9160. Free guide to stores on the State Street Mall.

Tourist Information Center State and Madison. Operates during summer months.

Emergency Numbers

Police; 911.
Fire; 911.

Poison Control Center; 942-5969.
Rape Help Line; 883-5688.

Helpful Numbers

Amtrak; (800) 972-9147 or 558-1075.
Chicago Bar Association; 332-1111. "Lawyer Reference Plan."
Chicago Convention & Tourism Bureau; 225-5000.
Chicago Motor Club; 372-1818. For driving directions.
Chicago Union Station; 346-5200.
City & Suburban Travel Information; (800) 972-7000.
Continental Air Transport; 454-7800. Buses to and from the airports.
Continental Trailways Bus Depot; 726-9500.
CTA Culture Bus Information; 836-7000.
Fine Arts Listings; 346-3278.
Greyhound Bus Lines; 346-5000.
Hot Tix Booth; 977-1755. Discount tickets.
Mayor's Office of Special Events; 744-3315.
O'Hare Airport Lost and Found; 686-2200.
Sports Phone; 976-1313.
Ticketron; 842-5387. Ticket service.
Time: 976-1616.
Visitor Event Line; 225-2323.
Weather; 976-1212.
Western Union; 435-0200.
Zip Codes; 886-2590.

JEWELRY SHOPS

C. D. Peacock 101 S. State (at Monroe); 630-5700. This is the oldest jewelry retailer in the city. The store has a Victorian atmosphere and some antique jewelry to go with it. High-quality modern merchandise, too.
Christian Bernard Water Tower Place, 835 N. Michigan; 527-1156. Branch of the Paris store.
Jewels by Stephanie 540 N. Michigan Avenue; 782-6300. Inside the Marriott Hotel. Stunning collection with stunning prices.
Lester Lampert 701 N. Michigan; 944-6888. Bold and creative.

Tiffany & Company 715 N. Michigan Avenue; 944-7500. The ultimate name. Jewelry, flatware, and china of impeccable quality; a few surprisingly modest prices, too.

Trabert & Hoeffer Jewels 940 N. Michigan Avenue; 787-1654.

LEATHER GOODS AND LUGGAGE

Chicago Trunk & Leather Works 12 S. Wabash; 372-0845. Big selection.

Greene's Luggage Water Tower Place, 835 N. Michigan; 337-3774. Well stocked. Repairs also done here.

Gucci 713 N. Michigan; 664-5504. High-priced status symbols.

Hermès Fashions 875 N. Michigan; 787-8175. Boutique inside Bonwit Teller.

I Santi Water Tower Place, 835 N. Michigan; 280-8398.

Leather Shop 191 W. Madison; 782-5448. Luggage and accessories—briefcases, wallets, checkbook covers.

North Beach Leather Water Tower Place, 835 N. Michigan; 280-9292. Trendy high-fashion leather clothes.

Tannery West Water Tower Place, 835 N. Michigan; 943-0908. Lots of Western wear.

LIMOUSINES

See TRANSPORTATION.

LINENS

Franklin Bayer Linen Shop 630 N. Michigan Avenue; 944-4737. Highest quality bed, bath, and table linens. Custom work.

M. Textrum Linens Water Tower Place, 835 N. Michigan; 642-8491. Table linens and accessories.

Scandia Down Shops 607 N. Wells; 787-6720. Fluffy down comforters and pillows with matching linens. Custom sewing and decorating available.

Shaxted 900 N. Michigan Avenue; 337-0855. Exquisite table and bed fittings, much custom work. Discontinued stock sold at 40 percent discount at Shaxted Annex, 300 W. Grand; 329-9660.

LINGERIE

Enchante Water Tower Place, 835 N. Michigan; 951-7290. Imported silks and designer items.

Underthings 804 W. Webster; 472-9291.

Whispers 2441 N. Clark; 327-4422. Wide selection of tasteful nightwear, lovely lingerie.

MAGIC AND METAPHYSICAL

Chicago Magic Center 19 W. Randolph; 726-2100.

El Sabarum's Religious Goods 3221 N. Sheffield; 248-0791. Occult supplies.

Occult Book Store 3230 N. Clark; 281-0599.

MOVIES

For the most complete movie listings, check Section Two of the *Reader*, a free weekly paper available in many retail stores. It lists capsule reviews for all films being shown in a given week—including those at university film centers. You can also check the daily entertainment sections of the *Tribune* and the *Sun-Times*.

Biograph 2433 N. Lincoln; 348-4123. Some foreign films, exclusive showings of unusual and hard-to-find movies. Special midnight shows Friday and Saturday.

Facets Multimedia Center 1517 W. Fullerton; 281-4114. Revival, unusual, and the off-beat.

Fine Arts 418 S. Michigan; 939-3700. Current foreign and art films.

Midwest Film Center Columbus Drive at Jackson; 443-3737. Behind the Art Institute, this center sponsors thoughtful retrospectives and premieres of important movies.

Music Box 3733 N. Southport; 871-6604. Lovingly restored, complete with organ, this "movie palace" changes its revival double features thrice weekly; weekend and some weekday matinees.

MUSEUMS

Most of the big museums of Chicago are open every day except Christmas and New Year's; the smaller ones are usually closed on Monday. Although hours and days are indicated here, it's best to call first; opening and closing hours can change. Many museums charge admittance. Those that don't or that offer "free days" are noted.

For museums outside of the downtown area, transportation information is given. This, too, is subject to change. For up-to-the-minute information, call the CTA (800) 972-7000. One of the best ways to cover the museum territory is the CTA Culture Bus, which runs every Sunday from mid-May through November. There are three different routes—north, south, and west—that hit almost every museum, special sight, and ethnic neighborhood. Your ticket is good all day.

The Culture Bus leaves from the Art Institute, Michigan Avenue at Adams. For more information, call 836-7000.

Art

Art Institute Michigan Avenue at Adams; 443-3500. This museum houses the most valued collection of French Impressionists in the United States. Also noteworthy are Chagall's stained-glass windows; the restored Louis A. Sullivan Trading Room from the Chicago Stock Exchange Building; and extensive selections in oriental art and modern paintings. There is also a Junior Museum for kids. Open Monday-Wednesday and Saturday, 10:30 A.M.–4:30 P.M.; Thursday, 10:30 A.M.–8:00 P.M.; Sunday, 12–5 P.M. Contribution required except on Thursday. Fantastic gift and book shop.

Martin D'Arcy Gallery of Art Cudahy Library at Loyola University, 6525 N. Sheridan; 274-3000. A medieval and Renaissance museum: art objects, enamel work, textiles, and creations in gold, silver, and ivory. Open 12–4 P.M., Monday and Friday; 6:30–9:30 P.M., Tuesday and Thursday; 1–4 P.M., Sunday. Admission free. Take the Howard el train north to the Loyola stop.

Museum of Contemporary Art 237 E. Ontario; 280-2660. The first exhibit is right outside; Claes Oldenburg's mural *Little Green Pills* graces one wall. Inside, this newly renovated and expanded museum houses both a permanent collection and changing exhibits. Open 10 A.M.–5 P.M., Tuesday–Saturday; Sunday, 12–5 P.M. Admission charge. Great gift shop.

Smart Gallery 5550 S. Greenwood; 753-2121. Part of University of Chicago campus, this new art gallery has Henry Moore drawings, a sculpture garden, the original Frank Lloyd Wright furniture from Robie House, plus a modern art collection. Open Tuesday-Saturday, 10:00 A.M.–4:00 P.M.; Sunday, 12–4:30 P.M. Closed university holidays and all of September. At State and Washington, take a southbound #6 bus to 55th and Hyde Park Boulevard. Transfer to #55 bus on 55th; get off at Greenwood.

Terra Museum of American Art 2600 Central Park, Evanston; 328-3400. A small gem of a museum devoted to 19th- and early 20th-century American art. Open Tuesday–Saturday, 11 A.M.–5 P.M., Sunday, 1–5 P.M.

Ethnic

The easiest way to get to these museums is to take the CTA Culture Bus. See TRANSPORTATION-PUBLIC or information at the beginning of MUSEUMS.

Balzekas Museum of Lithuanian Culture 4012 S. Archer; 847-2441. Open daily from 1–4:30 P.M. Monday free.
Polish National Museum 984 N. Milwaukee; 384-3352. Open daily from 1–4 P.M. Admission free.
Ukranian Institute of Modern Art 2247 W. Chicago; 384-6482. Open Tuesday–Saturday, 12–4 P.M., Sunday, 12–3 P.M. Admission free.
Ukranian National Museum 2453 W. Chicago; 276-6565. Open Tuesday–Saturday, 12–4 P.M.; Sunday, 12–3 P.M. Admission free.

Historical

Chicago Historical Society North Avenue at Clark; 642-4600. A Civil War gallery and Lincoln collection along with history of Chicago. The pioneer gallery puts on demonstrations of spinning, weaving, and candle dipping. Great costume collection. Open Monday–Saturday, 9:30 A.M.–4:30 P.M.; Sunday, 12–5 P.M.; Mondays free. From the Loop, catch a northbound Clark bus #22 or a Broadway bus #36 on Dearborn.
DuSable Museum of African-American History 57th & Cottage Grove; 947-0600. The history and art of black people. Open Monday–Friday, 9 A.M.–5 P.M.; Saturday, 1–5 P.M.; Sunday, 12–5 P.M. At State & Washington, take a southbound #6 bus to 55th and Hyde Park Boulevard. Transfer to the #55 bus on 55th; get off at Greenwood.

Spertus Museum of Judaica 618 S. Michigan; 922-9012. Rotating exhibits and a permanent collection reflecting Jewish life and culture. Open Monday–Thursday, 10 A.M.–5 P.M.; Friday, 10 A.M.–4 P.M.; Sunday, 1–4 P.M. Closed Saturday.

Scientific

Chicago Academy of Sciences 2001 N. Clark; 549-0606. Walk-through wildlife dioramas, replicas of coal forests and caves. Other natural history exhibits. Open every day from 10 A.M.–5 P.M. Admission free. From the Loop, catch a northbound Clark bus #22 or a Broadway bus #36 on Dearborn.

Field Museum of Natural History 1400 S. Lake Shore; 922-9410. Over 10 acres big, this fun museum is devoted to the sciences of anthropology, botany, geology, and zoology. Popular exhibits include: Hall of Dinosaurs; mummies; African Watering Hole; and the entire second floor, which is devoted to rare gems and jewels. Open every day but Christmas and New Year's, 9 A.M.–6 P.M. Fridays are free with a special late closing of 9:00 P.M. Pick up bus #126 (it's marked Planetarium) or bus #149 at Michigan & Jackson.

International Museum of Surgical Science & Hall of Fame 1524 N. Lake Shore Drive; 642-3632. This museum consists of 4 floors of showcases that detail the history of surgical and medical science. There's also a charming full-scale replica of an 1873 apothecary shop. Hours are 10 A.M.–4 P.M., weekdays and Saturday; 11 A.M.–5 P.M. on Sunday. Closed Monday. Free admission.

Museum of Science and Industry 57th & Lake Shore Drive; 684-1414. A top favorite. This is a participatory museum; go through a coal mine or a real German submarine or walk back through time on Main Street. All of this is housed in a restored building from the Columbian Exposition of 1893. Hours are 9:30 A.M.–5:30 P.M. daily. Free. Pick up a southbound Jeffrey Express bus #6 at State & Washington or an eastbound Drexel-Hyde Park bus #1 at Michigan & Washington.

Oriental Institute 1155 E. 58th; 753-2474. On the University of Chicago campus, it houses plunder from

MUSEUM OF SCIENCE AND INDUSTRY

Near Eastern, Egyptian, and Mesopotamian archae-
ological expeditions. Also, mummies and Dead Sea
Scrolls. Open 10 A.M.–4 P.M., Tuesday–Saturday; 12–
4 P.M., Sunday. Admission free. At State & Washington, take a southbound #6 bus to 55th and Hyde Park
Boulevard. Transfer to #55 bus on 55th; get off at
Greenwood.

Popular Culture and Miscellaneous

Adler Planetarium 1300 S. Lake Shore Drive; 322-
0300. Fantastic Sky Show, plus museum of antique
instruments. Some evenings the Doan Observatory is
open to public. Sky Shows at 11, 1, 2, 3, 4. Open from
9:30 A.M.–4:30 P.M. Pick up bus #126 (it's marked Planetarium) or bus #149 at Michigan & Jackson.
Bradford Museum of Collectors Plates 9333 N. Milwaukee, Niles; 966-2770. Over 1,000 limited-edition
collectors plates; current market values shown. Tours
can be arranged. Open 9 A.M.–4 P.M., weekdays; 10
A.M.–5 P.M., weekends.
John G. Shedd Aquarium 1200 S. Lake Shore Drive;
939-2426. The world's largest aquarium. Divers enter
the Coral Reef tank every day at 11 A.M. and 2 P.M. to
hand-feed fish. Open daily from 9 A.M.–5 P.M. Fridays
free. Pick up bus #126 (it's marked Planetarium) or
bus #149 at Michigan & Jackson.
Lizzardo Museum of Lapidary Art 220 Cottage Hill,
Elmhurst; 833-1616. Interesting museum devoted to
precious stones: jasper, jade, onyx, rose quartz, and
lapis are some of the gems displayed. Frequent demonstrations and educational programs. Open 1–5 P.M.,
Tuesday–Friday; 10 A.M.–5 P.M., Saturday; 1–5 P.M.,
Sunday. Fridays free.
Peace Museum 364 W. Erie; 440-1860. A combination
museum-cultural learning center dedicated to "peace
education through the arts." Changing art exhibits.
Hours are 1–7 P.M., Tuesday–Friday; 10 A.M.–4 P.M.,
Saturday. Admission free.
Telephony Museum & Art Gallery 225 W. Randolph;
727-2994. Operated by Illinois Bell. Includes historical
phones plus quiz games, electronics, and a small art
gallery. Open weekdays from 10 A.M.–4 P.M. Admission
free.

Museums

MUSIC

See also NIGHTLIFE.

Concerts and Clubs

For complete listings of musical concerts, check the listings in *Chicago* magazine or Section Two of the *Reader*, a free weekly publication available in many retail stores. Also, the *Tribune* and the *Sun-Times* carry many listings. Following is a selection of orchestras and clubs that present regular music concerts:

Classical

Chicago Chamber Orchestra 332 S. Michigan; 922-5570.
Chicago String Ensemble 410 S. Michigan; 786-0510.
Chicago Symphony Orchestra 220 S. Michigan; 435-8111. Featuring Sir Georg Solti.
Lyric Opera Civic Opera House, 20 N. Wacker; 346-6111.
Orchestra Hall 220 S. Michigan; 435-8111. Home to the Chicago Symphony and Sir Georg Solti, plus many other great visiting names. Friday matinees usually scheduled.

Country and Bluegrass

McGiddie's 2423 N. Lincoln; 472-7037. Bluegrass bands.
R R Ranch 56 W. Randolph; 263-8207.

Folk

Holsteins! 2464 N. Lincoln; 327-3331. One of the nation's premiere folk clubs, with a booking policy liberal enough to admit occasional country and pop acts.
Old Town School of Folk Music 909 W. Armitage; 525-7793. Along with lessons, the school hosts National Public Radio's "Flea Market" show and guest artists.

Jazz and Blues

Andy's 11 E. Hubbard; 642-6805. Jazz Monday through Friday.

Benchley's on Broadway 6232 N. Broadway; 973-6565. Jazz.

Biddy Mulligan's 7644 N. Sheridan; 761-6532. Reliable blues.

B.L.U.E.S. 2519 N. Halsted; 528-1012. Great blues every night.

Checkerboard Lounge 423 E. 43rd; 373-5948. The best of the blues.

Joe Segal's Jazz Showcase The Blackstone Hotel, 636 S. Michigan, 427-4300.

Kingston Mines 2548 N. Halsted; 477-4646. Blues every night, almost all night long. 4 A.M. closing.

Orphan's 2462 N. Lincoln; 929-2677. Blues and jazz.

Razzles Chicago Lake Shore Hotel, Lake Shore Drive & Ohio; 787-4700. Dixieland jazz.

Rick's Cafe Americain Holiday Inn - Lake Shore Drive, 644 N. Lake Shore; 943-9200. Big names in jazz.

Theresa's Lounge 607 E. 43; 285-2744. Chicago legend.

Wise Fools Pub 2270 N. Lincoln; 929-1510. Local blues and jazz.

Rock

Park West 322 W. Armitage; 929-5959. Elegant music club with varied schedule: rock, jazz, punk, reggae. Two-drink minimum. Tickets are often sold out in advance; check the box office or Ticketron, 842-5387.

Tuts 959 W. Belmont; 477-3365.

Wild Hare & Singing Armadillo Frog Sanctuary-A-Tavern 3530 N. Clark; 327-0800. Reggae seven nights a week.

Instruments and Sheet Music

Bein & Fushi Rare Violins 410 S. Michigan; 663-0150.

Carl Fischer 312 S. Wabash; 427-6652. Vast selection of sheet music.

Chicago Guitar Gallery 216 S. Wabash; 427-8434.

Folklore Center 407 W. Armitage; 528-1818.

CHICAGO TRIBUNE BUILDING
AND WEST FACADE OF THE WRIGLEY BUILDING

Graham Music Shop 17 N. Wabash; 263–1336. Band instruments.
Sound Post 1239 Chicago, Evanston; 866-6866.

Lessons

Chicago Conservatory College 410 S. Michigan; 427-0500.
Old Town School of Folk Music 909 W. Armitage; 525-7793.

NEWSPAPERS AND MAGAZINES

Chicago enjoys the reputation of a good newspaper town, unfortunately, several of the major papers have folded in recent years. There are only 2 major dailies left now:
Chicago Sun-Times Now owned by Rupert Murdoch, this paper is a flashy, energetic tabloid.
Chicago Tribune A more staid paper, with stronger "news" leanings. Now home to Chicago's favorite columnist, Mike Royko.

Weekly Newspapers

Crain's Chicago Business Well-reported, up-to-the-minute news on the local business community.
The Reader Chicago's "alternative" paper has magazine-style features and criticism. Section Two contains extensive listings: music, movies, theater, dance. Free; pick up Friday in various retail stores.

Magazines

Chicago Magazine Best known for its massive listings: music, art, kid stuff, lectures, dance, and the well-read restaurant guide. Monthly.
North Shore Magazine Features and listings pertaining to the exclusive North Shore suburbs. Monthly.

Other Papers

Chicago Daily Defender News and features pertaining to black interests.
Gaylife
Illinois Sports News
Lithuanian Daily News
Polish Daily Zgoda

NIGHTLIFE

See also BARS AND PUBS AND MUSIC.

Cabarets, Nightclubs, Dinner/Dancing

Backroom Club 1007 N. Rush; 944-2132. Jazz club and bar.
Bar of the Ritz Ritz-Carlton Hotel, 160 E. Pearson; 266-1000. Elegant cafe atmosphere; live music and dancing.
Baton Lounge 436 N. Clark; 644-5249. Las Vegas revue, with very professional female impersonators.
Bentley's 801 W. Willow; 280-9126. Wine bar.
Blue Max Hyatt Regency O'Hare, Rosemont; 696-1234. Nightclub with big-name entertainment.
Bulls 1916 N. Lincoln Park West; 337-6204. Basement club with live pop and jazz music.
Byfield's Ambassador East Hotel, 1301 N. State; 787-6433. Bar with live music and a fantastic, cheap buffet.
Crosscurrents 3206 N. Wilton (at Belmont); 472-7884. Cabaret with mix of jazz, satire, rock, and theater.
Embers 67 E. Walton; 944-1105. Popular, pleasant bar.
Empire Room Palmer House, State & Madison; 726-0330. Elegant, other-era nightclub.
Geja's Cafe 340 W. Armitage; 281-9101. Wine bar with classical guitar entertainment.
Greenhouse Bar Ritz-Carlton Hotel, 160 E. Pearson; 226-1000. Fantastic views and nice atmosphere.
Harry's Cafe 1035 N. Rush; 266-0167. Crowded, up-scale singles hangout.

La Cage Chicago 50 E. Oak; 944-3300. Campy night-club with male and female singers, plus female impersonators.

Playboy Club 1960 N. Lincoln Park West; 883-9090. Pasteurized sexy atmosphere; keys can be bought at the door for $25.

Rick's Cafe Americain Holiday Inn-Lake Shore, 644 N. Lake Shore; 943-9200. Top jazz cabaret.

Toulouse 49 W. Division; 944-2606. Classy restaurant with jazz bar.

Comedy Clubs

Chicago Comedy Showcase 1101 W. Diversey; 348-1101. Changing bill of improvs, stand-up comics, and companies.

Crosscurrents 3206 N. Wilton (at Belmont); 472-7884. Friday and Saturday nights belong to Aaron Freeman and his wild satires on local political life.

Second City 1616 N. Wells; 337-3992. Former home of Nichols and May, Dan Aykroyd, and John Belushi. Improvisational comedy revues.

Zanies 1548 N. Wells; 337-4027. Comedy featuring local and national talent.

Dance Clubs and Discos

Exit 1653 N. Wells; 440-0535. Rough and rowdy punk bar with dancing.

Hangge-Uppe 14 W. Elm; 337-0561. Three different bars plus two dance floors.

Neo 2350 N. Clark; 929-5501. Art Deco bar populated with David Bowie look-alikes. Jukebox dance floor.

Paradise 2848 N. Broadway; 871-1717. Considered the best dance hall in the city, with superb sound system.

Roxy 1157 W. Wrightwood; 472-8100. Lively cabaret with movie decor.

OBSERVATION POINTS

See SIGHTS WORTH SEEING.

PARKS AND NATURE PRESERVES

Garfield Park Conservatory 300 N. Central Park; 533-1281. Billed as "the world's largest horticultural conservatory." Admission free.

Grant Park East of Michigan Avenue from Randolph to Roosevelt Road. It's just a few steps from downtown skyscrapers to the beautiful gardens and foundations here. Free summer concerts in the band shell at night; during the day, a great view of the lake.

Ladd Arboretum 2024 N. McCormick Boulevard, Evanston; 864-5181. Hiking trails, bird sanctuary, prairies, and gardens.

Lincoln Park from North Avenue, 1600 N., to Foster Avenue, 5200 N. One of the most beautiful parts of the city: lagoons, running and biking paths, playgrounds, and squirrels. Encloses the zoo, conservatory, Chicago Historical Society, and the Chicago Academy of Sciences.

Lincoln Park Conservatory Fullerton & Stockton Drive (in Lincoln Park); 294-4770. Over 4 acres of flowers and plants. Shows change monthly. Admission free.

Shakespeare Garden Northwestern University, Garret Street and Sheridan Road, Evanston. A beautifully tended garden of flowers and herbs popular during Shakespeare's time.

PERFUME AND OTHER TOILETRIES

Caswell-Massey Water Tower Place, 835 N. Michigan; 664-1752. Authentic apothecary shop atmosphere. Imported perfume, soaps, bath gels, and lotions. Good brushes.

Les Parfums Des Century 2828 N. Clark; 525-9077. In the Century Shopping Mall. A well-stocked store with jewelry and accessories.
Les Parfums Shoppe 3017 N. Broadway; 935-0543. Modeled on Paris perfume shops.
Rare 'n Fair Water Tower Place, 835 N. Michigan; 266-9571. Another Parisian-style store.

PHOTOGRAPHY

For exhibits and shows, see ART GALLERIES.

Supplies and Equipment

Central Camera 230 S. Wabash; 427-5580.
Helix 325 W. Huron; 944-4400. A camera-lover's extravaganza—3 floors with a dozen different departments. Great mail order catalog.
Photo Center 875 N. Michigan; 337-4272.
Shutan Camera Company 153 W. Wacker; 332-2000.
Standard Photo 43 E. Chicago; 440-4920. Big, popular retail store. Cameras, accessories. Fast service on prints.
Wolk Camera 133 N. Wabash; 236-4425.

POLICE AND EMERGENCIES

Police; 911.
Fire; 911.
Ambulance; 911.

Poison Control Center; 942-5969.
Coast Guard Rescue; 768-8000.
Rape Help Line; 883-5688.

Police Department Information; 744-4000.

See also HOSPITALS & HEALTH EMERGENCIES, INFORMATION.

POLO
See SPORTS.

PRINTS AND POSTERS

Billy Hork Galleries 109 E. Oak; 337-1199.
Chicago Art Institute Michigan Avenue at Adams; 443-3536. Bookshop and gift store contains extensive poster and print collection.
Graphic Expectations 757 W. Diversey; 871-0957. Complete selection of film, theater, and advertising posters.
Poster Plus 2906 N. Broadway; 549-2822. Wide selection of art and advertising posters; some antiques.
Printworks, Ltd. 620 N. Michigan; 664-9407. Fine arts posters.

RACETRACKS

Arlington Park Euclid Avenue and Wilke Road, Arlington Heights; 255-4300. Flats. Open from late May to early December. Direct transportation available through the Chicago & Northwestern Station, 454-6677.
Hawthorne Race Track 3501 S. Laramie, Cicero; 652-9400. Flats. Open April to September. For transportation information, call CTA Travel Information (800) 972-7000, or (312) 836-7000.

Maywood Park North Avenue and 5th, Maywood; 626-4816. Trotters and pacers. Schedule varies. CTA Travel Information, (800) 972-7000, or (312) 836-7000.
Sportsman's Park 3301 S. Laramie, Cicero; 652-2812. Flats. Open April to September. For travel information, call (800) 972-7000, or (312) 836-7000.

RECORDS AND TAPES

Downtown Records on Rush 921 N. Rush; 649-9200 (plus 4 other locations). Lots of popular music.
Jazz Record Mart 77 E. Grand Avenue; 222-1467. Modern jazz, plus some rare 78s.
Laury's Discount Record Store 201 N. LaSalle; 263-3023. Broad selection of rock and classical. Good value.
Rizzoli's Water Tower Place, 845 N. Michigan; 642-3500. Imports department—classical, popular, rare.
Rose's Discount Record Store 165 W. Madison; 332-2737. Wide classical inventory, informed clerks. Usually can find some bargains.
Wax Trax 2449 N. Lincoln; 929-0221. Punk rock. Used records, also.

RELIGIOUS SERVICES

Consult the newspapers, especially on weekends, for times of services and other information.

RENTALS

Bicycles
Village Cycle Shop 1337 N. Wells; 751-2488. Rental

by the hour. Security deposit of $15 required; 5-hour minimum. Credit cards taken.

During summer months:

Rental stand at Navy Pier Grand Avenue and Lake Shore Drive. Bikes and roller skates rented here; security deposit required.
Rental stand in Lincoln Park Fullerton Avenue and Cannon. Right by the zoo. Bikes and roller skates available; security deposit required.

Boats

City Sailors 1461 W. Cuyler; 935-6145. Several 19-foot sailboats rented by the hour. Instructions available. Mid-May to October. No credit cards.
Lamprey Charter Boats 2520 N. Lincoln; 477-3555. A fishing-sailing charter that runs from mid-April to October. Advance reservations.
Paradise Yacht Sailing Charters P.O. Box 11390, Chicago 60611; 461-0666 (unit 5619). Luxury cruises on a 43-foot sailboat. Wining and dining included. From May to October.

Cars and Limos

See TRANSPORTATION.

Fishing Equipment

Chicago Sportfishing Association Burnham Park Harbor; 922-1100. Near south side lakeside park. Rents all lake fishing equipment. Boats also available.

Ice Skates

Daley Bicentennial Plaza 337 E. Randolph; 294-2493. Outdoor ice-skating rink during winter months. Very reasonable.

Roller Skates

Daley Bicentennial Plaza 337 E. Randolph; 294-2493. Outdoor roller rink in summer. Very reasonable.

During summer months:

Rental stand at Navy Pier Grand Avenue and Lake Shore Drive.
Rental stand in Lincoln Park Fullerton Avenue and Cannon.

Typewriters

If you're staying at a hotel, most typewriter rental agencies request that your hotel's concierge or guest service staff make the proper arrangements.

Mid-City Typewriter Exchange 22 N. Ada; 666-0745. No credit cards.

RESTAURANTS

All prices are based on a 3-course meal for 1 person. Tax, tip, and alcoholic beverages not included.
$ = under $10
$$ = $10–$25
$$$ = $30–$50
$$$$ = $50 and up
Always telephone to check on open days, hours, and reservations.

Loop

Berghoff 17 W. Adams; 427-3170. German; no credit cards. Old World and Chicago tradition here; great weiner schnitzel, saurbraten, and thuringers or broiled steaks or fish. Men's Grill—bar and carved sandwiches—now serves women, too. Closed Sunday. ($)
Bev' n' Bob's Deli 67 E. Adams; 939-2100. Breakfast, lunch, early dinner. Closed Sunday. ($)
Binyon's 327 S. Plymouth Court; 341-1155. Lots of prime rib, steaks, lobsters. House specialty is turtle soup. Crowded and noisy. Closed Sunday. ($)
Cart 601 S. Wabash; 427-0700. Open until 1:30 A.M. Prime rib and seafood. ($$)

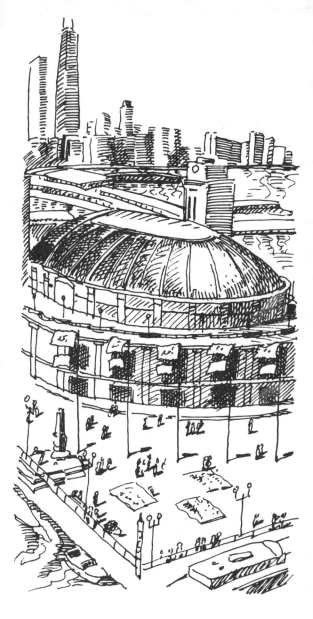

NAVY PIER

Empire Room Palmer House, State and Monroe; 726-0330. Closed Sunday and Monday. Noted more for its atmosphere than cuisine. ($$$)

Federal Inn 323 S. Federal; 939-3590. Weekdays only. Continental menu. ($$)

Gene & Georgetti 500 N. Franklin; 527-3718. Steaks. Regulars usually get seated first; average waiting time in the packed bar is over an hour. Still, it's a popular place and the steaks are unbeatable. Closed Sunday. ($$$)

Italian Village 71 W. Monroe; 332-7005. Three restaurants here: the expensive Florentine Room; moderate Village; and small, intimate La Cantina. Popular with theatergoers. ($$—$$$)

Knossos 180 N. LaSalle; 236-2442. Weekdays. Greek-American. ($)

Le Bordeaux 3 W. Madison; 372-2027. French bistro atmosphere and food. ($)

Loophole 59 E. Randolph; 236-6242. Great soups and sandwiches. ($)

Lou Mitchell's 565 W. Jackson; 939-3111. Breakfast and lunch. Closed Sunday. The wait here is always worth it. Opens at 5:30 A.M. ($)

Mayor's Row on Dearborn 131 N. Dearborn; 332-0224. Weekdays only. Good steak and potatoes fare. ($$)

Mort's Deli 159 N. Wabash; 236-9566. Monday through Friday, 7 A.M.–6:50 P.M.; Saturday, 8:00 A.M.–5 P.M. Good corned beef. ($)

Nick's Fishmarket 1 First National Plaza; 621-0200. Closed Sunday; no lunch Saturday; jacket requested. Flashy, expensive seafood place. High quality. ($$$$)

Sign of the Trader 141 W. Jackson; 427-3443. Weekdays. Inside the Board of Trade building; ticker tapes click during lunch. ($)

Truffles 151 E. Wacker Drive; 565-1000. French nouvelle. Jackets required. Fantastic food, fantastic atmosphere, fantastically high prices. ($$$$)

Near North

Acorn on Oak 116 E. Oak; 944-6835. Famous for its hamburgers; English pub setting. ($)

Arnie's 1030 N. State; 266-4800. Popular with out-of-towners, Arnie's is decorated in art-deco-plus. Known for fish and pasta dishes. ($$$–$$$$)

Bastille 21 W. Superior; 787-2050. French bistro. ($$)

Bigg's 1150 N. Dearborn; 787-0900. Dinner only. Victorian mansion; continental prix fixe menu. ($$$$)

Billy Goat Tavern 430 N. Michigan; 222-1525. Home of Saturday Night Live's famous "chezburger, chezburger." Popular with reporters. ($)

Billy's 936 N. Rush; 943-7080. Dinner only; closed Sunday. Italian specialties; crowded bar. ($$)

Blackhawk on Pearson 110 E. Pearson; 943-3300. Closed Sunday. Prime rib and seafood. ($$)

Boccaccio's 153 E. Erie; 944-2450. Closed Sunday. Italian; antipasto bar. ($)

Bon Ton 1153 N. State; 943-0538. Hungarian cooking plus fantastic pastry. ($)

Cape Cod Room Drake Hotel, Lake Shore Drive and Michigan; 787-2200. Seafood. Reservations almost always needed. ($$$)

Cafe Angelo 225 N. Wabash; 332-3370. Dozens of regional Italian choices. Open for breakfast, lunch, dinner weekdays; dinner only Saturday; closed Sunday. ($$)

Cafe Jaspar 105 E. Ontario; 642-5404. Closed Sunday. Classy cafeteria during the day; tablecloths, waiters, and a different menu at night. ($)

Carson's 612 N. Wells; 280-9200. Famous for its ribs; first choice rib house of both *Chicago* magazine and the *New York Times*. Long lines; no reservations. ($$)

Chapman Sisters Calorie Counter 444 N. Michigan; 329-9690. Fun cafeteria even for those not on diets. Lots of health foods. ($)

Chestnut Street Grill Water Tower Place, 835 N. Michigan; 280-2720. Fresh seafood; extensive California wine list. ($$$)

Chez Paul 660 N. Rush; 944-6680. Coat and tie required. French cuisine in a Victorian mansion. ($$$$)

Corona Cafe 501 N. Rush; 527-5456. Steaks and Italian. Good food; if you're willing to give up some atmosphere, go around the corner for counter service. The menu's the same; the prices considerably lower. ($$)

Cricket's 100 E. Chestnut; 280-2100. Continental menu. Based on New York's "21" Club. ($$$$)

D. B. Kaplan's Deli Water Tower Place, 835 N. Michigan; 280-2700. Over 150 wild sandwiches. ($)

Don the Beachcomber 101 E. Walton; 787-8812. Polynesian. ($$)

Don's Fishmarket & Raw Bar 1123 N. State; 943-2800. Fresh fish flown in daily. Slick, modern decor. ($$$)

Don Roth's River Plaza 405 N. Wabash; 527-3100. California-style atmosphere and food. Popular during lunchtime with reporters from the *Sun-Times.* Closed Sunday. ($)

Doro's 871 N. Rush; 266-1414. Northern Italian. Very slow paced. ($$$)

Eli's the Place for Steak 215 E. Chicago; 642-1393. Jackets required. Noisy, crowded; top quality steaks. ($$$)

Embers 67 E. Walton; 944-1105. Prime rib. ($$$)

Eugene's 1255 N. State; 944-1445. Damon Runyon-gangster motif; steaks, prime rib, seafood. Great chocolate mousse. ($$$$)

Gordon 512 N. Clark; 467-9780. Closed Monday. Continental. Accomplished cuisine, chic decor; no kids. ($$$)

Hamburger Hamlet 44 E. Walton; 649-6600. Dark, cozily cluttered atmosphere; great hamburgers, chili, steak, salads, and omelettes. ($)

Hillary's Water Tower Place, 835 N. Michigan; 280-2710. Good appetizers and hamburgers; friendly bar scene. Inside Water Tower Place. ($$)

Hippo 50 E. Oak; 944-3300. French bistro; outdoor tables in the summer. ($$)

Houlihan's 1201 N. Dearborn; 642-9647. Fun atmosphere; creative menu. ($)

Ireland's 600 N. LaSalle; 337-2020. Seafood. ($$)

Johnny's 161 E. Huron; 943-2828. Closed Sunday. Continental menu. ($$)

Jovan's 1660 N. LaSalle; 944-7766. Saturday dinner only, closed Sunday; no kids. Takes only American Express and Diner's Club cards. Gourmet French prix fixe dinners. ($$$$)

Kinzie Steak House 33 W. Kinzie; 644-7470. Steaks and ribs. ($$)

Lawry's—the Prime Rib 100 E. Ontario; 787-5000. Prime rib only for dinner; slightly expanded lunch menu. ($$)

L'Escargot 701 N. Michigan; 337-1717. Good French food at less-than-expected prices. ($$)

Le Mignon 712 N. Rush; 664-1033. Closed Sunday. Continental dining in a turn-of-the-century townhouse. ($$)

Le Perroquet 70 E. Walton; 944-2990. Coat and tie

required; no kids; closed Sunday. American Express and Diner's Club. French nouvelle cuisine; fixed-price lunch is $15.75, dinner is $35.75. Considered one of the city's very best restaurants. Fantastic service, food, and setting. ($$$$)

Magic Pan 60 E. Walton; 943-2456. Crêpes. ($)

Maine Lobster House 22 E. Chestnut; 787-3976. Dinner only, low-key place with fresh seafood. ($$)

Morton's 1050 N. State; 266-4820. Dinner only; closed Sunday. Steaks and seafood; huge portions. No menus or visible prices. ($$$)

Palm 181 E. Lake Shore Drive; 944-0135. Steaks. Chicago version of New York favorite; casual, fun atmosphere. ($$$$)

Pronto 200 E. Chestnut; 664-6181. Homemade pasta; large portions. ($$)

Pump Room 1301 N. State; 266-0360. No denim. Popular with celebrities, whose pictures line the walls. Crisp, 1930s nightclub decor. ($$$)

Riccardo's 437 N. Rush; 944-8815. Closed weekends. Italian-American. Packed with newspaper reporters, ad men, artists, and TV personalities. The food is not as lively as the crowd; try egg lemon soup and green noodles al forno. Lunch in café upstairs. ($$)

Sages on State Street 1255 N. State; 944-1557. Closed Sunday. Steak and seafood in plush Victorian trappings. ($$)

Service Entrance 215 E. Chestnut; 787-4525. Closed Sunday. Charming little place with soups, salads, sandwiches. ($)

Sherlock's Home 126 E. Delaware; 787-0545. Looks like an English pub; fun place for coffee, brandy, and dessert. ($$)

Shuckers 150 E. Ontario; 266-6057. Closed Sunday. Seafood and raw bar in low-key surroundings. ($$)

Sweetwater 1028 N. Rush; 787-5552. Caters to celebrities, athletes, and singles. Art deco setting; some tables with view of Rush Street. ($$$)

Tale of the Whale 900 N. Michigan; 944-4798. Dinner only. Seafood in New England village environment. ($$)

Tambourine 200 E. Chestnut; 944-4000. Good, pleasant offerings; ribs, lots of chicken, salads, and seafood. ($)

Toulouse 51 W. Division; 944-2606. French. Elegant

bistro combined with sophisticated piano bar. Thoughtful service. ($$$)

Waterfront 1015 N. Rush; 943-7494. Seafood. Casual dining spot with fantastic gumbo. ($$)

Wrigley Building Restaurant 410 N. Michigan; 944-7600. Closed weekends. American. Men's club atmosphere; hearty, quality food. ($$)

Old Town-Lincoln Park-Lakeview

Ambria 2300 N. Lincoln Park West; 427-5959. Jackets required; no denim, no kids. One of Chicago's best. Graceful, understated dining room; fixed-price of $35 or lots of daily specials. ($$$$)

Ann Sather's 925 W. Belmont; 348-2378. A favorite restaurant of everyone's. Good, homecooked food—including some Swedish dishes—at low prices. Breakfast, lunch, early dinner. ($)

Bakery 2218 N. Lincoln; 477-6942. Continental prix fixe around $30. ($$$)

Bentley's 801 W. Willow; 280-9126. Wine bar and café with light, sophisticated food. ($$)

Bowl & Roll 1339 N. Wells; 944-5361. Homemade soup and sandwiches. ($)

Chicago Claim Company 2314 N. Clark; 871-1770. Super, big hamburgers. ($)

Geja's 340 W. Armitage; 281-9101. Fondue, wine and cheese. ($)

Gitanes 2350 N. Clark; 929-5500. Continental menu. ($$)

Jerome's 2450 N. Clark; 327-2207. Creative menu, fantastic baked goods. Outdoor café in summer. Always crowded. ($$)

La Creperie 2940 N. Clark; 528-9050. Crêpes Breton-style; very popular place. ($)

La Fontaine 2442 N. Clark; 525-1800. Closed Monday. Jackets required. Truly elegant, intimate place with classic French cuisine. Wine list tends to up the bill. ($$$–$$$$)

Lawrence of Oregano 662 W. Diversey; 871-1916. Italian cuisine, great salad bar. ($)

Mel Markon's 2150 N. Lincoln Park West; 525-5550. Spiffy deli. Open very late, usually to 4:00 or 5:00 A.M. ($)

R. J. Grunts 2056 N. Lincoln Park West; 929-5363. Wildly creative menu. ($)

Tango 3172 N. Sheridan; 935-0350. Starkly sophisticated setting; seafood is the specialty. ($$)

That Steak Joynt 1610 N. Wells; 943-5091. Plush turn-of-century trappings; lots of steaks. ($$$)

Un Grand Café 2300 N. Lincoln Park West; 348-8886. French bistro atmosphere plus exquisite food. Popular with celebrities. ($$$)

Pizza

Chicago is famous for its deep-dish pizza—over an inch thick and manageable only with a knife and a fork. All restaurants listed here are ($)

Alferno's 2916 N. Broadway; 528-9165.

Bacino's 2204 N. Lincoln; 472-7400.

De Brucio's 845 N. Michigan; 951-6777. No credit cards. Sells deep-dish by the slice.

Gino's East 160 E. Superior; 943-1124. American Express only.

Giordano's 747 N. Rush; 951-0747. No credit cards. Also has a stuffed pizza.

Pizzeria Due 619 N. Wabash; 943-2400. No credit cards.

Pizzeria Uno 29 E. Ohio; 321-1000. No credit cards; closed Sunday and Monday.

Ranalli's 1925 N. Lincoln; 642-4700.

Ethnic

Chinese

House of Hunan 535 N. Michigan; 329-9494. Hunan, Sichuan, Mandarin; unbeatable cuisine. ($$)

Lee's Canton Cafe 2300 S. Wentworth; 225-4838. ($)

Man-Dar Inn 2130 S. Wentworth; 842-4014. ($)

German

Golden Ox 1578 N. Clybourne; 664-6780. ($)

Schwaben Stube 3500 N. Lincoln; 528-1142. Bavarian-style food. ($)

Zum Deutschen Eck 2924 N. Southport; 525-8389. ($$)

Greek

Dianna's 212 S. Halsted; 332-1225. A Chicago favorite, this restaurant is behind a Greek grocery store. Open until 2 A.M. ($)

Greek Islands 200 S. Halsted; 782-9855. Busy, popular family-style place. Good value. Open every day. ($)

Parthenon 314 S. Halsted; 726-2407. Greek food, music, dancing. Open until 1:30 A.M. ($)

Roditys 222 S. Halsted; 454-0800. ($)

Indian

Family Corner 2901 W. Devon; 262-2854. Famous for its Indian vegetarian pizza. ($)

Gaylord 678 N. Clark; 664-1700. Good tandoori. ($$)

Japanese

Benihana 166 E. Superior; 664-9643. Chop-and-flash Japanese cooking at the table. Parties of less than 6 have to share tables. ($$)

Fuji Restaurant 76 W. Lake; 368-0052. Great, inexpensive Japanese food; especially good tempura. Closed Sunday. ($)

Hana East 210 E. Ohio; 751-2100. Japanese food cooked at your table; 10 people to a table. ($$)

Happy Sushi 3346 N. Clark; 528-1225. Just like its name; other entrees, too. ($)

Hatsuhana 160 E. Ontario; 280-8287. Authentic Japanese food. There's a long sushi bar. ($$)

Ron of Japan 230 E. Ontario; 644-6500. Steakhouse, Japan-style. ($$)

Shino 18 E. Huron; 944-1321. Closed Sunday. Japanese seafood; elegant decor. ($$)

Korean

Garden of Happiness 3450 N. Lincoln; 348-2120. ($)

Korea House 3301 N. Clark; 348-3480. ($)

Poolgogi Steakhouse 1334 W. Morse; 761-1366. ($)

Mexican

La Canasta 1007 W. Armitage; 975-9667. Great Mexican food at very reasonable prices. ($)

La Cantina 29 W. Division; 642-2400. Mexican to eat in or take out. ($)

La Margarita 868 N. Wabash; 751-3434. ($)

Meson Del Lago 158 E. Ontario; 649-9215. Stylish Mexican restaurant with popular taco bar. ($)

Su Casa 49 E. Ontario; 943-4041. Closed Sunday. Mild Mexican delights in villa setting. ($$)

Middle Eastern

Casbah 514 W. Diversey; 935-7570. Armenian menu with lots of choices. ($$)

Sayat Nova 157 E. Ohio; 644-9159. Armenian cuisine. ($)

Russian

Kavkaz 6405 N. Claremont; 338-1316. Closed Monday. Georgian dishes. ($)

South American

El Criollo 1706 W. Fullerton; 549-3373. Argentinian fare. ($)

El Inca 6221 N. Broadway; 262-7077. Peruvian menu. ($)

Piqueo 5427 N. Clark; 769-0455. Full-course Peruvian meals. ($$)

Thai

Bangkok House 2544 W. Devon; 338-5948. ($)

Thai Little Home Cafe 3125 W. Lawrence; 478-3944. ($)

Vietnamese

Dalat 1020 W. Argyle; 728-0288. The newest ethnic cuisine in town is Oriental with a French touch.

Brunch

This category usually applies to Sunday only.

Arnie's 1030 N. State; 266-4800. Huge all-you-can eat buffet. ($$)

Cricket's 100 E. Chestnut; 280-2100. Emphasis on Creole fare. ($$)

Gitanes 2350 N. Clark; 929-5500. Four courses; good omelettes. ($$)

Jacques' Garden 900 N. Michigan; 944-4795. Charming New Orleans garden setting. ($$)

La Creperie 2940 N. Clark; 528-9050. Delicious crêpes and omelettes. ($)

Magic Pan 60 E. Walton; 943-2456. Crêpes. ($)

Mel Markon's 2150 Lincoln Park West; 525-5550. Lox, bagels, omelettes. ($)

Pump Room 1301 N. State; 266-0360. À la carte. ($$)

R. J. Grunts 2056 Lincoln Park West; 929-5363. Popular for brunch; lots of choices. ($)

Late Closings

Acorn on Oak 116 E. Oak; 944-6835. Open until 4 A.M. ($)

Bagel Nosh 1135 N. State; 266-6369. Open 24 hours. ($)

Carson's 612 N. Wells; 280-9200. Open until midnight weekdays; 1 A.M. Friday and Saturday. ($$)

Mel Markon's 2150 N. Lincoln Park West; 525-5550. Closes at 4 A.M., 5 A.M. weekends. ($)

Oak Tree Restaurant 25 E. Oak; 751-1988. No credit cards. Never closes. ($)

Pump Room 1300 N. State; 266-0360. Open until 2 A.M. ($$$)

Ritz-Carlton Cafe 160 E. Pearson; 266-1000. Open 24 hours. ($$)

Open-Air

Azteca Cafe 215 W. North; 944-9854. Wonderful outdoor courtyard in summer; Mexican food. ($$)

Ciao 1516 N. Wells; 266-0048. Delicate Northern Italian cuisine; outdoor café in the summer. ($$)

Hemingway's Movable Feast 1825 Lincoln Plaza; 943-6225. Hundreds of sandwich combinations, salads, good desserts. Outside cafe in the summer. ($)

Lutz 2458 W. Montrose; 478-7785. European café renowned for its pastries. Also, light meals. Outdoor café. ($)

Melvin's 1116 N. State; 664-0356. No credit cards. Hamburgers and an outdoor café. ($)

With a View

Ninety-Fifth 172 E. Chestnut; 787-9596. Nouvelle cuisine. On the 95th floor of the John Hancock Building; very gracious atmosphere. Lower priced Sunset Menu in early evening. Also Sunday brunch. ($$$$)
Sweetwater 1028 N. Rush; 787-5552. Some people-watching tables look out at Rush Street. ($$$)

Worth the Trip to the Suburbs

Alouette 440 Green Bay Road, Highwood; 433-5600. French cuisine, graceful antique furnishings. ($$$)
Cafe Provencal 1625 Hinman, Evanston; 475-2233. Well-known French provincial menu. ($$)
Cottage 525 Torrence, Calumet City; 891-3900. Thoughtful continental menu; emphasis on fresh ingredients. ($$$)
Kwality India 954 W. Lake, Oak Park; 848-1710. Both northern and southern cuisines; over 30 entrees. ($)
Le Francais 269 N. Milwaukee, Wheeling; 541-7470. Award-winning French cuisine. Impeccable service, style. ($$$$)

ROLLER SKATES

See RENTALS.

SECOND-HAND CLOTHING/THRIFT-VINTAGE

Entre-Nous 21 E. Delaware; 337-2919. Resale designer clothes.
Fashion Exchange Center 67 E. Oak; 664-1657. Good fashionable resales.

Second-Hand Clothing

Finders Keepers 2467 N. Lincoln; 525-1510. Resale shop run by private school. Nice clothes for low prices.
La Bourse 45 E. Walton; 787-3925. Charity-run resale shop. Antiques, furniture, dishes, silver. No clothes.
Mysel Furs 6 E. Monroe; 372-9513. Recycled furs.
Service League Thrift Shop 54 W. Chicago; 664-8164 or 337-8266. Run by hospital league. Gigantic, 2-floor resale shop: clothes, furniture, silver. Great buys.

SHOES

Athlete's Foot Water Tower Place, 835 N. Michigan; 642-8881. Or 330 S. Michigan; 663-1464. Shoes for all sports.
Bally of Switzerland 909 N. Michigan; 787-8110. Also, 116 S. Wabash; 782-2106. Quality imports. Expensive.
Charles Jourdan Water Tower Place, 835 N. Michigan; 280-8133. Shoes from Paris; very fashionable.
Gucci 713 N. Michigan; 664-5504. Very expensive, top-quality shoes for men and women.
Joseph Salon Shoes 50 E. Randolph; 332-2772. Also, 679 N. Michigan; 944-1111. Designer names like Maud Frizon. Good bargains in basement.
Smyth Brothers 33 E. Oak; 664-9508. Also, Water Tower Place, 835 N. Michigan; 642-7798. High-fashion shoes.
Todd's Boots 5 S. Wabash; 372-1385. Good bargains on Frye boots.

SHOPPING MALLS AND CENTERS

Off-Center 300 West Grand at Franklin; 321-9500. A high-tech warehouse that's been converted to a discount shopping mall. Every store offers at least 25 percent off merchandise often seen in Michigan Avenue stores.

State Street Mall State Street from Wacker Drive to Congress; 782-9160. "That great street" is lined with Chicago's major department stores, plus movie theaters, restaurants, and specialty stores. For a free guide, stop at the State Street Council, 36 S. State.

Water Tower Place 835–845 N. Michigan; 440-3368. This spectacular atrium shopping mall is home to over 110 stores, 4 cinemas, and 10 restaurants. Branches of Marshall Fields and Lord & Taylor are there, too. Many boutiques are quality, unique places. The perfect inside window-shopping delight.

SIGHTS WORTH SEEING

See also MUSEUMS, PARKS AND NATURE PRESERVES.

Architectural Sights

Chicago is famous for its architecture. When the Great Fire of 1871 leveled the downtown area, the city was rebuilt by many famous names: Louis H. Sullivan, Holabird & Root, Mies van der Rohe; Frank Lloyd Wright lived and worked here. Here are some of the prime examples of the Chicago School of Architecture:

Archicenter 330 S. Dearborn; 782-1776. Operated by the Chicago Architecture Foundation, this center has complete information on Chicago architecture. Tours, including "Chicago Loop Walk," regularly scheduled. A book and gift shop, plus exhibits. Open Monday–Friday, 9:30 A.M.–5:30 P.M.; Saturday, 9 A.M.–3 P.M.

Auditorium Building 430 S. Michigan; 922-2110. A landmark building designed by Adler & Sullivan in 1889. Inside, original, beautiful stencilling has been completely restored. Tours for those with keen preservationist or architectural interests. Reservations required.

Carson Pirie Scott & Company Building 1 S. State

Street. Beautifully restored Louis H. Sullivan façade and foyer.

Crown Hall I.I.T. Campus, 3360 S. State. Has been called Mies van der Rohe's masterpiece.

860–880 Lake Shore Drive Apartments Designed by Mies van der Rohe, these steel and glass buildings have been copied all over the world.

Federal Center Complex 219 S. Dearborn. Designed by Mies van der Rohe; Alexander Calder "stabile", *Flamingo*, in courtyard across street.

First National Bank Building & Plaza 38 S. Dearborn. The world's tallest bank. Plaza contains Marc Chagall mosaic murals, *Four Seasons*, and the Hamal Fountain. From May to September, the plaza has a café and free concerts during the week.

Frank Lloyd Wright Historic District Oak Park Visitors Center, 158 N. Forest, Oak Park; 848-1978. A major concentration of the architect's work. Walking tours, exhibits, and information. Take the CTA Lake Street El, West Line, to Oak Park.

Gage Building 18 S. Michigan. Famed Louis H. Sullivan façade.

IBM Building 1 IBM Plaza (opposite the *Sun-Times* at 401 N. Wabash). Designed by Mies van der Rohe and C. F. Murphy Associates in 1971, it looks like a gigantic keypunch card.

Inland Steel Building Dearborn & Monroe. Designed by Skidmore, Owings, & Merrill.

John Hancock Center 875 N. Michigan. Third-tallest skyscraper in the world.

Madlener House 4 W. Burton Place. Prototypical "city house" built in 1902; a designated Chicago landmark.

Marina City Towers 300 N. State. Corncob twin towers are a well-known city symbol. Built in 1963 by Bertrand Goldberg Associates.

Marquette Building 140 S. Dearborn. Chicago-style architecture with lovely mosaics lobby.

Monadnock Building 53 W. Jackson. Once the world's tallest office building, this is a noted Chicago landmark.

Prairie Avenue Historic District 1800 block of S. Prairie. Restored cobblestone street of mansions once inhabited by Chicago society. Includes *Glessner House*, 1800 S. Prairie; 326-1393. Built in 1886 for a Chicago industrialist, it now houses the Chicago School of Architecture Foundation.

ROBIE HOUSE BY FRANK LLOYD WRIGHT

Reliance Building 32 N. State. Built in 1895 by D. H. Burnham & Co., this building was considered an architectural breakthrough. Notice terra-cotta moldings.

Robie House 57th & Woodlawn; 753-4420. The prototypical Prairie House, designed by Frank Lloyd Wright in 1909. Listed on the National Register of Historic Places. Interior shown by appointment only.

Rookery Building 209 S. LaSalle. A Chicago landmark that's also on the National Register of Historic Places. The oldest remaining steel-skeleton skyscraper was built in 1886 by Burnham & Root; the breathtaking lobby was remodeled in 1905 by Frank Lloyd Wright.

Sears Tower Wacker Drive at Adams. Tallest building in the world.

Standard Oil Building 200 E. Randolph. World's tallest marble-faced building. A wind-activated sculpture on lower level.

Tribune Tower 435 N. Michigan. A Gothic landmark built, after a famous design contest, in 1925. This is home to the *Tribune* newspaper. Tours run Monday to Saturday; call 222-3993 for reservations.

Water Tower 800 N. Michigan (at Chicago). One of the few buildings to survive the Great Chicago Fire of 1871. Inside the Gothic fortress tower of sandstone is a Tourist Information Center.

Churches

Baha'i House of Worship Sheridan and Linden, Wilmette; 256-4400. Breath-taking 9-sided white dome is a center for Baha'i followers. Ornate architectural style, with intricate scroll work. Open 10 A.M.–10 P.M.; special tours by appointment only.

Chicago Loop Synagogue 16 S. Clark; 346-7370. Built in 1963. Metal sculpture. *The Hands of Peace* by Henri Azaz, above door; visitors' balcony inside with view of stained glass window by Abraham Rattner.

Chicago Temple 77 W. Washington; 236-4548. Chicago's oldest church.

Fourth Presbyterian Church 125 E. Chestnut; 787-4570. A prime example of neo-Gothic style, this church was built in 1912. Note the carved Bedford stone and beautiful stained-glass windows.

Holy Name Cathedral 730 N. Wabash; 787-8040. Center for the largest archdiocese in the United States. Originally built in 1874, it's been remodeled twice since.

Holy Trinity Orthodox Cathedral 1121 N. Leavitt. Designed in 1903 by Louis H. Sullivan.

Rockefeller Memorial Chapel 5850 S. Woodlawn; 753-3381. On University of Chicago campus; neo-Gothic design.

St. Chrysostom's Church 1424 N. Dearborn; 944-1083. Beautiful stained-glass windows. Tours arranged.

Second Presbyterian Church 1936 S. Michigan. Stained-glass windows by Tiffany; Mrs. Abraham Lincoln worshiped here.

Seventeenth Church of Christ Scientist 55 E. Wacker; 236-4671. Marbled circular dome designed by Weese & Associates in 1968.

Historical Sights

Jane Addams Hull House Halsted at Polk; 663-2793. Located on the University of Illinois Circle Campus, this is the restored home-community center of the famous social worker. A National Historic Monument.

Other Landmarks

Anti-Cruelty Society 157 W. Grand; 644-8338. Designed by Stanley Tigerman, this whimsical building looks like a dog's face on the outside; inside, animals live in white gazebos and kitten or puppy nurseries.

Apparel Center 350 N. Orleans. Fashion-trade showrooms. Varying public hours; some bargains and closeouts. See BARGAIN AND DISCOUNT STORES.

Art Clubs of Chicago 109 E. Ontario; 787-3997. Interior design by Mies van der Rohe; various exhibitions mounted.

Atrium Houses 1370 W. Madison Park. Windowless houses designed by Y. C. Wong, student of Mies van der Rohe.

Bach House 7415 N. Sheridan. Designed by Frank Lloyd Wright.

Dewes House 503 W. Wrightwood. Also known as the Swedish Engineers Society, this is a startling eclectic mix of designs. Built in 1896.

Fine Arts Building 410 S. Michigan. A designated Chicago landmark, this building was erected in 1885; the architect, Solon S. Berman, also designed the Pullman community.

Law School Building 1121 E. 60th Street. On University of Chicago campus, a "corrugated" building by Eero Saarinen.

Merchandise Mart 350 N. Wells. Built by the Kennedys, this is the largest 1-building wholesale center. This is where top-flight furniture companies have their showrooms; however, unless you have identification showing you are a buyer or decorator, you won't be admitted. Tours are available; see TOURS & SIGHTSEEING.

Old Colony Building 407 S. Dearborn. Distinctive round towers; architects Holabird and Roche.

Pullman Community 111th Street and Champlain. The first planned industrial community in this country, built in the 1880s.

Site of the Origin of the Great Chicago Fire DeKoven & Jefferson. *Pillar of Fire* sculpture marks the beginning of the 1871 fire that destroyed the city.

Union Stockyard Gate Exchange Avenue and Peoria. 1875 limestone gate is all that's left of the once-famous stockyards.

Wrigley Building 410 N. Michigan. This white terracotta building with the big clock is a Chicago favorite. Built in 1921, it's beautifully lighted at night.

Outdoor Art

Arris SE Corner of Congress and Dearborn. Sculpture by John Henry.

Batcolumn 600 W. Madison. 101-foot outdoor sculpture by Claes Oldenburg.

Flamingo Federal Center Plaza, Monroe and Dearborn. Alexander Calder "stabile."

Fountain of Time Washington Park, west of Cottage Grove Avenue. Mammoth sculpture (over 100 figures) passing before Father Time. By Lorado Taft.

Four Seasons First National Plaza, 38 S. Dearborn. Marc Chagall mosaic murals.

Miro's Chicago Washington between Clark and Dearborn.

Pablo Picasso sculpture Daley Center Plaza, between Clark and Dearborn at Washington.

Special Neighborhoods

Alta Vista Terrace 1050 W. Grace. One block of homes based on those in Victorian London. Each house has a mirror image on the opposite side of the street. A Chicago landmark.

Astor Street 50 E. from 1200 N. to 1600 N. Beautiful old mansions; street named after John Jacob Astor.

Chinatown 22nd and Wentworth. Two-block shopping district: restaurants, grocery stores, small shops of handicrafts.

Printing House Row S. Dearborn from W. Congress Parkway to W. Polk. "Adaptive re-use" means converting industrial buildings, such as these former printing plants, into fashionable loft-style apartments; bookshops, restaurants, art galleries, and the like will follow, as they have here.

Views

John Hancock Center Observatory 875 N. Michigan; 751-3681. Take in the view from the world's third-tallest building: 94 floors and 1,030 feet up. Visibility varies according to the weather (60 miles is the maximum); daily visibility posted before you go up. Open 9 A.M.–midnight.

Sears Tower Skydeck Wacker Drive at Adams; 875-9696. The tallest building in the world; you can't quite see forever—it just looks that way. The skydeck is 103 floors and 1,353 feet high. Visibility posted on ground floor. Open 9 A.M.–midnight.

Other Chicago Sights

Board of Trade Building 141 W. Jackson; 435-3626. Spectacular building with elaborate art deco lobby.

Ceres, Roman goddess of agriculture, is the statue on the top. Inside, the biggest and rowdiest commodities futures market in United States. Free tours: Monday–Friday at 9:15, 10:15, 11:00, 11:45 A.M., and 12:30 P.M.

Buckingham Fountain Grant Park at Congress Parkway. Patterned after the Latona Fountain in Versailles, this one was erected in 1927. Major displays every day from late May through September; color displays in evenings between 9–10 P.M.

Chicago Mercantile Exchange 444 W. Jackson; 648-1000. Lots of fun observing the antics of the world's largest perishable commodities exchange. Visitors' gallery open Monday–Friday 9 A.M.–1 P.M.

Chicago Public Library & Cultural Center 78 E. Washington; 269-2900. This 1897 building used to be the central library; now it's been restored for use as a cultural center. A must-see: Tiffany glass dome and chandeliers; marble staircases; rare woods and mosaics. Beautiful rooms for reading, rest, or a rendezvous. Free lunchtime concerts during summer.

Graceland Cemetery 4001 N. Clark; 525-1105. Notable Chicagoans are buried here beside often startling architecture. Marshall Field, Allan Pinkerton, George Pullman, Mies van der Rohe, Cyrus McCormick. Pyramids, copies of Greek temples, and tombs by Louis H. Sullivan. Maps available. Open 8 A.M.–8 P.M.

SPECIALTY STORES

A Show of Hands 43 E. Walton; 943-3413. Clever crafts, many handmade.

Accent Chicago Water Tower Place, 845 N. Michigan; 944-1354. Tasteful souvenirs (some expensive) of the Windy City.

Animal Accents 56 E. Walton; 787-5446. Gifts featuring animals in some way, shape, or material.

Beagle & Company Water Tower Place, 835 N. Michigan; 337-8000. Snoopy and friends.

Beauty & the Beast Water Tower Place, 835 N. Michigan; 944-7570. Antique dolls, unusual stuffed animals.

City 213 W. Institute Place; 664-9581. Breathlessly chic designs, high-tech and postmodern, in everything from chairs to clothes to toothbrushes. There's even a café, Monique's, adjacent.

Clark & Barlow 353 W. Grand; 726-3010. The ultimate hardware store.

Emporium 1551 N. Wells; 337-7126. Beautiful kites sold right next to Lincoln Park.

Erotic Cakes 248-8831. A bakery is being built; until then, they deliver X-rated goodies.

Goodie's 3450 N. Halsted; 477-8223. Just for fun: trinkets and toys with a '50s flavor.

He Who Eats Mud 3247 N. Broadway; 525-0616. Sophisticated and campy paper goods, knickknacks.

Illinois Theatrical Footwear Company Stevens Building Arcade, 17 N. State; 332-7123.

Jade House 700 N. Michigan; 266-0911. Jade jewelry and carvings.

Joy's Clock & Telephone Shops Water Tower Place, 845 N. Michigan; 664-1531. Expensive and novelty clocks and phones.

La Boîte a Musique Water Tower Place, 835 N. Michigan; 944-2227. Music boxes in all sizes and tunes.

Lady Madonna Maternity Boutique Water Tower Place, 835 N. Michigan; 266-2420. Stylish clothes for mothers-to-be and their offspring.

Le Sportsac Water Tower Place, 835 N. Michigan; 266-9635. Outlet for good-looking nylon luggage and travel kits.

Mark & Lois Jacobs Americana Collectibles 2465 N. Lincoln; 935-4204. Lots of political memorabilia, movie posters, pop culture.

Nonpareil 2300 N. Clark; 477-2933. The ultimate cunning little shop: fashion, jewelry, whimsical pottery, toys, paper goods.

Tivoli Gardens 2262 N. Clark; 477-7710. Paper goods, mechanical toys, baskets, jewelry.

Toperie Water Tower Place, 835 N. Michigan; 266-0991. Quality personalized and monogrammed goods: T-shirts, book bags, sweaters.

Universal Pen Hospital Stevens Building Arcade, 17 N. State; 332-5373. Repairs of all kinds; some new stock.

Specialty Stores

SOCCER

See SPORTS.

SPORTING GOODS

Eddie Bauer 123 N. Wabash, 263-6005. Quality outdoor wear and equipment. Also at Water Tower Place.
Herman's World of Sporting Goods 111 E. Chicago; 951-8282. Sportswear and equipment.
Morrie Mages 620 N. LaSalle; 337-6151. Multi-floor store has everything from roller skates to sweat-bands to electric socks. Lots of fun.
Port Supply 2245 S. Michigan Avenue; 842-2704. Everything for sailboats and yachts. Machine accessories.

SPORTS

For the latest news and scores, call: *Sun-Times*; 943-3080
Tribune; 222-1234
Sports Phone; 936-1313.

Baseball

Chicago Cubs; 248-7900.
Home games are played at Wrigley Field, Clark and Addison. At this writing, it's the last "old-time" (1914) park in the majors—no night games, ivy growing on the walls.

Chicago White Sox; 924-1000.
Home games played at Comiskey Park, 35th and Dan Ryan Expressway. For advance reservations, call 225-5769.

Basketball

Chicago Bulls; 346-1122.
Home games played at Chicago Stadium, 1800 W. Madison. Tickets also available through Ticketron, 454-6777.

Football

Chicago Bears; 663-5408.
Home games at Soldier Field. Tickets available through Ticketron, 454-6777, or the Box Office at 55 E. Jackson.

Hockey

Chicago Black Hawks; 733-5300.
Home games at Chicago Stadium, 1800 W. Madison. Tickets also available through Ticketron, 454-6777.

Polo

Oak Brook Polo Club.
In the summer, the club plays in the International Sports Core, 1000 Oak Brook Road, Oak Brook. Call 654-1500. The indoor season is played at the Onwentsia Club in Lake Forest. Call 234-6220.

Soccer

Chicago Sting; 558-5425.
Playing field can vary. Tickets available through Ticketron, 454-6777, or Box Office, at 333 N. Michigan.

Transportation

Check with the CTA, 836-7000, for specific directions. All sports events can be reached through public transportation; the CTA can give you exact instructions. In the spring, several restaurants run package deals of brunch and a trip to the ballpark. In the fall, a brunch-football game is the package. Check with Sweetwater, 1028 N. Rush, 787-5552.

See also RACETRACKS.

STATIONERY

Business
Business Stationers, Inc. 919 N. Michigan; 664-3030.
Horders 111 W. Adams; 648-7208. Also, 69 W. Washington; 648-7203. And 149 E. Ohio; 648-7200. King of office supply.
Utility Stationery Stores 25 S. Wabash; 782-0490.

Personal
Metcalfe's 664 N. Dearborn; 337-6646. Grande dame of engraved stationery. Famous for its wedding invitations.
Watermark 912 N. Michigan; 664-3203. Personal and designer note paper; personalized everything—stationery, invitations, party favors, ribbons.
Write Impressions, Ltd. 42 E. Chicago; 943-3306. Casual and formal stationery, gift wrappings, party needs. Many personalized goods.

TAXIS
See TRANSPORTATION.

THEATERS

For the most current theater listings, check the arts sections in the Sunday papers (Arts/Books in the *Tribune*, Show in the *Sun-Times*) or Section Two in the *Reader*, a free weekly paper found in many book and record stores. *Chicago* magazine often gives capsules of plays' plots. Or call the League of Chicago Theaters, 977-1730, for information.

CHICAGO TOWER

Tickets can be obtained through the theater box offices, either in person or by phone if you're paying with a credit card. Also, try Ticketron, 200 N. Michigan; 454-6777. This is a computerized ticket service that charges a small fee.

Discount tickets can be obtained at the **Hot Tix Booth**, at the Daley Center Plaza, Washington and Clark. It offers half-price tickets on the day of performance. Hours are Tuesday–Friday, 11 A.M.–6 P.M.; Saturday, 10 A.M.–5 P.M. Tickets for Sunday and Monday performances can be bought on Saturday. You can pick up a free theater guide and schedule there.

Theaters in Chicago tend to fall into 3 groups: Loop, Off-Loop, and Off-Off-Loop. These categories refer not strictly to location but types of productions as well. Loop theaters tend to run big productions with name stars or road shows—*Chorus Line, Annie, Evita*, or Carol Channing or Katherine Hepburn starring, or Tom Stoppard directing. Off-Loop features Chicago's finest actors, playwrights, and directors in original material or revivals. Off-Off tends to be more experimental or avant-garde.

Loop

Arie Crown McCormick Place, E. 23rd and Lake Shore Drive; 791-6000. A 5-minute taxi ride from downtown.
Blackstone 60 E. Balbo; 977-1700.
Goodman 200 S. Columbus; 443-3800.
Shubert 22 W. Monroe; 977-1700.

Off-Loop

Apollo Theater Center 2540 N. Lincoln; 935-6100.
Body Politic Theatre 2261 N. Lincoln; 871-3000.
Court Theatre 5535 S. Ellis; 753-3581.
Free Shakespeare Theatre 1608 N. Wells; 271-6190.
Huron Theater 1608 N. Wells; 266-7055.
Kuumba Theatre 218 S. Wabash; 461-9396.
North Light Repertory 2300 Green Bay Road, Evanston; 869-7278.
Old Town Players 1718 N. North Park; 645-0145.
Organic Theater Company 3319 N. Clark; 327-5588.
Pegasus Players 1020 W. Bryn Mawr; 271-2638.

Remains Theatre 1034 W. Barry; 549-7725.
Second City 1616 N. Wells; 337-3992. Former home of many famous comedians, including several of the *Saturday Night Live* crowd; satirical revues, six nights a week.
Steppenwolf 2851 N. Halsted; 472-4141.
Story Theatre 1608 N. Wells; 787-5259.
Travel Light 1225 W. Belmont; 281-6060.
Victory Gardens 2257 N. Lincoln; 871-3000.
Wisdom Bridge 1559 W. Howard; 743-6442. Take the El to the Howard stop.

Off-Off Loop

Black Ensemble Theater 1655 N. Burling; 751-0263.
Chicago City Theatre Company 410 S. Michigan; 663-3618.
Chicago Comedy Showcase 1055 W. Diversey; 348-1101.
Chicago Premiere Society 1548 N. Wells; 977-1700.
Horses, Inc. 2857 N. Halsted; 327-8373.

THINGS TO DO

Chicago Transit Authority Culture Bus 836-7000. Ride the Culture Bus to museums and ethnic neighborhoods. Operates every Sunday from mid-May to November. See TRANSPORTATION for information.
Jardine Water Purification Plant 1000 E. Ohio; 744-3692. Free tours of the world's biggest water-purifying facility. Weekends every hour on the hour from 1–4 P.M.
Kitchens of Sara Lee 500 Waukegan Road, Deerfield; 945-2525. Tour of the bakery plant; samples served afterwards. Reservations required.
Lamprey Charter Boats 2520 N. Lincoln; 477-3555. A fishing-sailing charter that runs from the middle of April to October. Advance reservations.

Maxwell Street Halsted Street and 1320 South. A Chicago institution of buying, trading, and haggling in the open street. It's seen finer days, but go on a Sunday morning and be prepared to be accosted by zealous street merchants. Prices are to be dickered over, of course.

Northwestern University Dearborn Observatory 2131 Sheridan Road, Evanston; 492-7651. Weather permitting, every Friday night, small groups are allowed to tour observatory and view celestial objects through the telescope. Write ahead stating desired date.

Paradise Alternative P.O. Box 11390, Chicago, 60611; 726-9420, unit 5619. Take a luxury cruise on a 43-foot sailboat. Wining and dining included. From May to October; 24-hour notice.

U.S.S. Silversides Navy Pier, E. Grand and Lake Michigan. This moored submarine is open for visitors 12–6 P.M. daily.

Water Tower Place 835 N. Michigan. Fabulous 7-story atrium shopping mall filled with trendy and expensive boutiques, restaurants, and cinemas.

TOBACCO

Alfred Dunhill of London Water Tower Place, 835 N. Michigan; 467-4455. Finest quality cigars and cigarettes.

Iwan Ries & Company 17 S. Wabash; 372-1306. Large selection of pipes and pipe tobacco.

Monroe Cigar Company 180 N. LaSalle; 236-6143. Also, Merchandise Mart Plaza; 644-7308. And 24 N. Wabash; 782-4189. Imported and domestic cigars. Pipe repair. Over 30 other downtown locations.

Old Chicago Smoke Shops 169 N. Clark; 236-9771. Free delivery.

333 Tobacco Shop 333 N. Michigan; 782-4317. Specializes in hand-rolled cigars.

Tinder Box Water Tower Place, 835 N. Michigan; 943-4475.

Up Down Tobacco Shop 1550 N. Wells; 337-8505. Loose cigarette tobacco, Canary Islands cigars, selection of pipes.

TOURS AND SIGHTSEEING

American Sightseeing International 530 S. Michigan; 427-3100. A choice of 9 different tours of the city: Chinatown After Dark, Old Town, Nightclubbing, All-Day Metropolitan, etc.

Archicenter 330 S. Dearborn; 782-1776. Run by the Chicago Architecture Foundation, Archicenter offers walking, bike, and bus tours that center on unique architectural sights.

Chicago À La Carte 664 N. Michigan; 440-1276. Popular with people who are considering moving or have just moved here. Focuses on neighborhoods, schools, housing, community activities: what Chicago can offer a newcomer. Limousine service.

Chicago Helicopter Airways 5240 W. 63rd; 735-0200. For lots of bucks, a 4-passenger helicopter can fly you over the Loop and Near North area, back by the lakeshore. One-week notice usually.

Chicago Historical Society Clark Street and North Avenue; 642-4600. A variety of interesting walking tours.

Coach Horse Livery 951-9520. Hire liveries and a driver for a tour of Near North streets. Loads on Chestnut Street side of John Hancock Building, 7 P.M.–2 A.M. For 2–8 people.

Glessner House 1800 S. Prairie; 326-1393. Restored 1886 mansion row houses the Chicago School of Architecture Foundation. Museum, library, and information center. Open Tuesday, Thursday, Saturday, 10 A.M.–2 P.M.; Sunday 1–5 P.M. Take bus #1 (marked Drexel-Hyde Park) from Washington and State to Michigan and 18th. Walk east.

Gray Line Tours 400 N. Wabash; 329-1444. Operates out of various hotels; a dozen various tours.

Jane Addams Hull House Halsted at Polk; 668-2793. Located on the University of Illinois Circle campus, this is the restored home-community center of the famous social worker. A National Historic Monument. Tours daily.

Merchandise Mart/Apparel Center 325 N. Wells; 661-1440. Public tours, Thursdays 10 A.M.–1:30 P.M.

Mercury Sightseeing Boats SW corner of Michigan Avenue Bridge; 332-1353. Operates from late spring to early fall. Choice of lake and river trips for varying lengths of time.

Oak Park Tour Center 158 N. Forest Avenue, Oak Park; 848-1978. Tours of Frank Lloyd Wright houses and works by other Prairie School architects. Accessible by public transportation.

On the Scene Tours 205 W. Wacker Drive; 661-1440. Tours of Merchandise Mart/Apparel Center, which are usually closed to public. Also can arrange group tours of city.

Sun-Times 401 N. Wabash; 321-2032. Behind the scenes of a major daily paper. Call for reservations.

Tribune Tower 435 N. Michigan. Home of the *Tribune* newspaper, this building is a gothic landmark. Tours run Monday to Friday, 9:30 A.M., 11 A.M., 1:15 P.M., and 2:45 P.M.; Saturday at 9:30 A.M., 12, and 1:15 P.M. Reservations required; call 222-3993.

Wendella Sightseeing Boats 400 N. Michigan; 337-1446. From the foot of the bridge by the Wrigley Building. Goes along Chicago River and out onto the lake. From April 15 to September 15.

TOYS

Beagle & Company Water Tower Place, 835 N. Michigan; 337-8000. Peanuts characters: Snoopy and all his friends; accessories.

Beauty & the Beast Water Tower Place, 835 N. Michigan; 944-7570. Every breed of stuffed animal resides here.

F. A. O. Schwarz Water Tower Place, 835 N. Michigan; 787-8894. Big exotic toy store stuffed with unusual choices. Tends to be expensive, but some not-so-dear items, too.

Gamesters Water Tower Place, 835 N. Michigan; 642-0671. An adult toy store (you must be 16 years old to enter). Board games, trains, practical jokes.

Saturday's Child 2146 N. Halsted; 525-8697. Large store with interesting selection: imports, dolls, games, knick-knacks, books.

Stuart Brent Bookstore 670 N. Michigan; 337-6357. Educational toys on lower level.

TRAINS

See TRANSPORTATION.

TRANSPORTATION

Arrivals & Departures

Airports

O'Hare International Airport At this writing, it is possible to reach the airport via a rapid-transit/bus combination that takes between 60 and 90 minutes from downtown, at a cost of $1 one-way. Taxis from O'Hare to the city are plentiful but expensive. Continental Air Transport buses leave every 15 minutes outside of each terminal. The buses will take you to the Loop, South Loop, North Loop, or Gold Coast hotels. The buses also stop at train and bus stations, the Sears Tower, and the Merchandise Mart. Approximate cost is $3.50. To get to O'Hare, pick up a bus at various hotel stops. Call Air Transport for details: 454-7800.

Midway Airport This airport often feels like a ghost town, but it's very convenient to the downtown area. Continental Air Transport buses go to several downtown and Near North hotels. Departures are approximately every hour. To get to Midway, catch the bus at the Westin, Drake, Palmer House, Conrad Hilton hotels, or call Air Transport, 454-7800. Taxis can be found in front of Midway or you can try the #62 Archer Express bus across from the terminal. Fares, at this writing, are 90¢ exact change. No dollar bills accepted.

Bus Stations

Continental Trailways 20 E. Randolph; 726-9500.
Greyhound Lines Randolph and Clark; 346-5000.
Both stations are in the Loop, close to public transportation and taxis.

Train Station

Chicago Union Station 210 S. Canal; 346-5200. Arrival and departure point for Amtrak trains. Short taxi ride from Near North area; walking distance (if not too loaded down) from Loop. Taxis in front of station.

Car Rental

Most agencies can be found at either O'Hare or Midway Airports. All take major credit cards. Book ahead for weekends.

Avis 201 N. Dearborn; 630-8943. 1030 N. State; 642-2049.
Budget 200 N. Dearborn; 580-5151.
Econo-Car 3121 N. Broadway; 281-6544.
Hertz 225 N. Dearborn; 372-7600.
National Car 191 N. Dearborn; 236-2581.

Limousine Rental

Al & Harold Golub Limo Service 188 W. Randolph; 726-1035.
Gold Coast Limousine 2430 W. Belden; 588-8000. No credit cards, but will bill companies.
Rush Street Limousine 32 W. Randolph; 332-0226. Can also provide armed bodyguards.
We Chauffeur, Inc. 1 American Plaza, Evanston; 328-5650. One-day notice for a chauffeur to drive your car.

Public Transportation

Chicago public transportation consists of buses and el trains. ("El" stands for elevated, although some of the trains become subways downtown.) Both are run by the financially beleagured Chicago Transit Authority (CTA) and both can be wonderfully convenient or a real burden. Try to avoid during rush hours.

Buses require exact change (90¢ at this writing, 10¢ for a transfer) and dollar bills are not acceptable. The els are usually the fastest way to get somewhere, but—as in all big cities—are not always the safest way to travel alone, late at night.

CTA maps are free and can be picked up at any Chicago Public Library or the Library's Cultural Center, 78 E. Washington. Maps also available at the Mayor's Office of Inquiry in City Hall; information booths at 160 N. LaSalle or in the Daley Center, between Clark and Dearborn at Washington.

For exact directions on how to get somewhere, call the Travel Information Line, (800) 972-7000. It operates around-the-clock.

The CTA Culture Bus runs every Sunday from mid-May through November. There are 3 different routes—north, south, and west—that hit almost every museum, special sight, and ethnic neighborhood. Your ticket is good all day; ride awhile, get off and explore a museum, then get back on again. The Culture Bus leaves from the Art Institute, Michigan and Adams. For Culture Bus information, call 836-7000.

Taxis

Taxis can be easily found unless it's raining or snowing. They operate on the meter system, starting at $1.00.

American United Cab; 248-7600.
Checker Taxi; 666-3700.
Flash Cab; 561-1444.
Fleet Medicate Service; 928-5006. Transportation for the handicapped.
Jiffy Cab; 487-9000.
Yellow Cab Company; 225-6000.

To the Suburbs

If you're not driving, the best access to the suburbs can be found through the commuter railroads. Stations located in the Loop. The Regional Transportation Authority Information Center, 836-7000, can help you find the correct commuter line, train station, and times.

Chicago & Northwestern Station West Madison and North Canal; 454-6677. Lines to the North Shore, northwest, and west suburbs.
Illinois Central Gulf Station 151 N. Michigan Avenue; 332-0295, (800) 972-7000. Southern suburbs and south sides of the city (59th, 63rd, 67th, and 115th Sts.).
LaSalle Street Station LaSalle & Van Buren; 435-7300.

UNIVERSITIES

Columbia College 600 S. Michigan. Known for its energetic fine arts departments. For Dance Center information, call 663-1600. The Theater/Music Center number is 663-9462.
Northwestern University Sheridan and Chicago, Evanston. Many cultural activities, including an extensive film board program and musical concerts at Pick-Staiger Hall. A monthly calendar of events is available at 663 Clark, Evanston.
University of Chicago 5801 S. Ellis. The campus contains many museums—the Smart Gallery and the Oriental Institute (see MUSEUMS for details), plus other fascinating buildings. Foremost is Rockefeller Memorial Chapel, the Gothic masterpiece that dominates the campus. Many examples of classic modern architecture, also. (See SIGHTS TO SEE—ARCHITECTURE.) Frank Lloyd Wright's Robie House is on campus, too. Also, America's oldest student-run film society—Doc Films—operates here. For film listings, call 753-2898.

University of Illinois at Chicago 601 S. Morgan (University Hall, Main Administration Building). Sprawling campus comprises the former U. of I. Chicago Circle (with its famous, futuristic buildings) and the U. of I. Medical Center. Main information number is 996-3000.

WEATHER

It's said if you don't like the weather here, just wait a few minutes—it'll change. Temperatures can drop or rise 30 degrees in 1 hour and the wind-chill factor can make it feel 20 to 30 degrees colder than the actual recorded temperature.

In the winter, Chicago is famous for its snow. Temperatures average 8–33 degrees Fahrenheit in January. Winter necessities include warm clothes (preferably layers) and coat, gloves, hats, and waterproof boots.

April can be rainy and chilly; in June, temperatures start to climb. High humidity marks the summer months; average temperatures for July include highs of 85 to 90 degrees Fahrenheit, lows of 67 to 70.

Weather Report; 976-1212

WINES AND LIQUORS

Bragno Wines & Spirits, Ltd. 40 E. Walton; 337-5000. No credit cards.

House of Glunz 1206 N. Wells; 642-3000. Well-known wine store. Big stock of imported and domestics. Credit cards taken.

LaSalle Street Market 745 N. LaSalle; 943-7450. Big selection of wines and champagnes. Also, gourmet deli. Credit cards taken.

Sam's Liquors 1000 W. North; 664-4394. Seedy exterior; fantastic selection and prices inside. Quality choices. Deliveries.
Stop & Shop 233 E. Wacker; 853-2160; also, 260 E. Chestnut; 853-2155; and 1313 Ritchie Court; 853-2150. Gourmet groceries with good selections of wines and liquors. Deliveries; credit cards.

WOMEN'S INTERESTS

See also GAY SCENE.

Bookstores

Barbara's Bookstore 1434 N. Wells; 642-5044. 2907 N. Broadway; 477-0411.
Women & Children First 1967 N. Halsted; 440-8824.

Information and Counseling

Chicago Women's Counseling Collective 372-5560.
Flexible Careers 37 S. Wabash; 236-6028. Career development service.
Midwest Women's Center 53 W. Jackson; 922-8530. A complete educational referral and service center.
Rape Victims Help Line 883-5688.
Women Against Rape 372-6600.
Women Employed 5 S. Wabash; 782-3902. Research center concerning problems and issues facing working women.

ZOOS

Brookfield Zoo 8400 W. 31st, Brookfield; 242-2630. A major zoo. Special attractions include Australia House—complete with a Tasmanian Devil and wombats; a baboon island; spectacular Dolphin Show; a trained walrus; and many African animals. Open from 10 A.M.–6 P.M. during the summer, 10 A.M.–5 P.M. in winter. Tuesdays free.

John G. Shedd Aquarium 1200 S. Lake Shore Drive; 939-2426. Over 5,000 fish, including sharks and eels. Special 90,000-gallon Coral Reef tank where divers hand-feed fish. Open every day but Christmas and New Year's, 9 A.M.–5 P.M. Fridays free.

Lincoln Park Zoo 2200 N. Cannon Drive (in Lincoln Park); 294-4660. Small zoo that is currently undergoing some renovation. Brand new Penguin House, Farm in the Zoo, modern Ape House, and beautiful nature walks through the Rookery. Open every day 9 A.M.–5 P.M. Admission free.

MAPS

Downtown Chicago

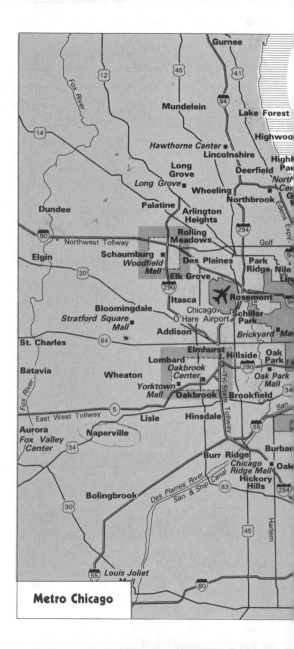

Metro Chicago

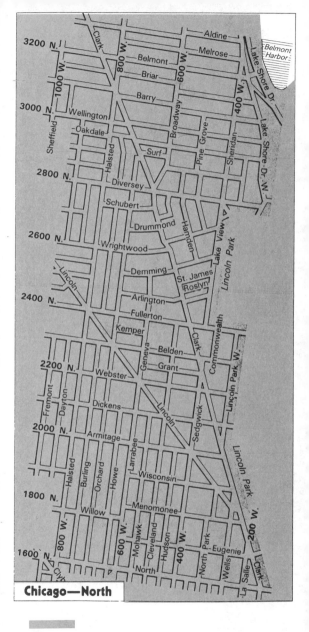

Chicago—North

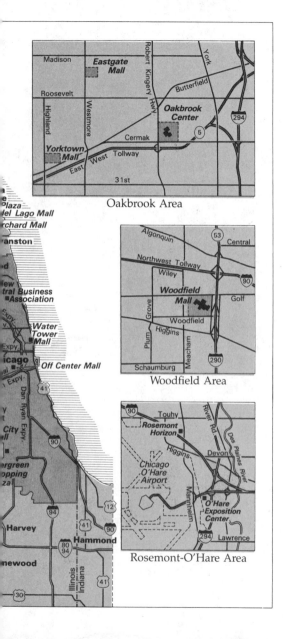

Oakbrook Area

Woodfield Area

Rosemont-O'Hare Area